ADDICT
TO
ACADEMIC

RECOVERY FROM 30 YEARS OF DRUG ADDICTION

By John E. Smethers, Ph.D.

ADDICT TO ACADEMIC: Recovery From 30 Years Of Drug Addiction
ISBN-13: 978-1-906628-50-5

Published by CheckPoint Press, Ireland
www.checkpointpress.com

This book is dedicated to my grandchildren

Kayla and Jeren Castenada

Table of Contents

FOREWORD

Most addicts would like to recover from a life of chaos caused by the rigors of drug and/or alcohol addiction, but most don't have the wherewithal to accomplish it. I believe in a process, although I wasn't aware of it prior to writing this book. This process, you might say, is the brainchild of this book, but it's not a new idea. Books have been written about journaling, and it's a tool used by many counselors to enhance the lives of their clients. Socrates said that an unexamined life is not worth living.

Writing a history of one's life can and often does serve as an impetus for recovery. It'll also serve as a map into the territory we call experience and memory, showing where we and others have traveled, and leading into areas of human experience that are so essential to this journey we call life. I expect, as has been the case for me, that along the way many others can and/or will uncover lost and forgotten pieces of themselves. In the process, perhaps they'll discover hidden places within their souls that are wellsprings of healing and life.

Like a compass, a life history can only point in one direction. If those who try writing it are anything like me, they'll want to make what's left of their lives more meaningful than their pasts. All one has to do is take the first step. Once this journey is embarked upon, change, to some degree, is inevitable and the writers will in unexpected ways feel themselves turning into different people.

Writing a life history may be one of the most personal and intimate processes we can do. Through our personal history we can come to know who we are in new and unforeseen ways. We can also reveal to others what is deepest in out hearts, and in the process build bridges. The very act of sharing a personal history contradicts the isolation that characterizes the lives of so many addicts. A life history carries within it the seeds of community, and because life histories take time and patience to write, they often serve as potent antidotes to depression, self-loathing, and demoralization. Without a past, we have no place to stand, no place from which to see, and no clear direction for our future actions.

A life history for addicts becomes the vehicle through which we organize the events that happen to us. It's also our way of telling time. Our life history takes shape like chapters in a book, each in its proper place, one following the next, explaining why events happened as they did, lending logic to our decisions and bringing meaning to what would otherwise be a collection of drunkalogues or drugalogues. Without life histories, life becomes a book cover without the pages—nice to look at, but not very meaningful.

At the end of our lives, after we've passed on, all that's left are our life histories. In a unique and fascinating way, these life histories are our ticket to immortality. Knowing that future generations will read and retell our stories, and knowing that other recovering addicts will read and be inspired by them, is—at least for me a consolation that warrants merit.

Starting such a project can be daunting, however, so the best way to proceed is to incorporate what I refer to as automatic writing. That is, just start writing, whether there's a plan in mind or not. Write something, anything, just to get started, and keep writing for thirty minutes. It doesn't matter whether the words makes sense, whether the ramblings are grammatically incorrect, or whether there are misspelled words—just keep writing without stopping—not even for two seconds. Once there's a chunk of text visible, a life history, which can end up in the form of a book, has been started. Then it can be edited.

In the beginning, it was hard for an addict like me to gather memories that were obliterated from so many years of drug and alcohol addiction, so I used my police record as a guide. My arrest record spans 30 years and I have three different copies of it—one from the sixties, one from the eighties, and a recent one. Another device that helped was my employment record from the Social Security Administration. With those tools, I was surprised how much I started re-membering.

If we could open up the mind like the hood of a car, the task would be much simpler. While experience is encoded by all the senses, the primary fuel that triggers our memory is often pictorial. However, there are exceptions. I, for one, think in words, but most people rely on other senses for their principal knowledge of our world. Regardless of a person's learning orientation, research confirms that for most people, it's the *image* of past events that are most accessible to recollection.

Each time we journey inward and trace the path of a memory to its origins, we seem to discover nuances and connections that were previously unnoticed.

The illumination of our current awareness is also conditioned by our emotional state and by seemingly trivial matters such as the aroma of a former lover or the sound of familiar music, thereby filtering the process of recall. For example, the smell of a used book store can open a door to a whole realm of past experience that I haven't considered for years. I might see myself standing next door to an old book store with a friend I haven't thought of for years. A former girlfriend's beautiful face suddenly intrudes on this memory. Her touch metamorphoses into my grandmother's dainty fingers stroking my hair. My mind wanders through a multitude of images and warm feelings (or perhaps cold feelings). With addicts, there are often as many negative feelings coming over us as the warm ones. Whatever the feelings and images are, they are the fuel—the words needed for a life history.

By allowing ourselves to be purposefully drawn inward, something remarkable happens. Our past merges with the present, permitting us to reclaim and recreate something formerly hidden. Moving against the tide of the present, however, requires a conscious decision, an act of will to re-member.

The following pages are my life history, and I begin at the end with memories of the past—the end being the Ph.D. that I earned after more than 30 years of drug and alcohol addiction, over 40 arrests, and five formal probations, all culminating with time spent in the state penitentiary.

Advisory: Readers are respectfully advised that for the purposes of maintaining the originality and integrity of this autobiographical story, this book contains language, and depicts scenes and activities that may not be suitable for younger readers.

CheckPoint Press

CHAPTER ONE

The Third Day

I have literally beaten the odds and shouldn't be here writing these words on my computer. I should've been dead many times over but I'm not. It is my hope that my experiences of going from addict to academic will give others the incentive to know that total abstinence from chemical substances is possible for anyone, regardless of the pits of despair, their drug of choice, and of the number of years they've used drugs.

As I sat with my classmates at the graduation commencement for my doctorate, waiting for my name to be called, I couldn't help thinking about the way my life was during the last few years of my addiction when I was a bartender.

~

A bar called California Country in Barstow got a lot of patronage from my bartending. Although I was inexperienced at mixing drinks, I was a good bartender, in the sense that a lot of people kept coming back because I entertained them with stories from my past and with my warped sense of humor. Although I was forty years old, that was my first job as a bartender in 20 years, so sometimes I'd have to ask customers how to mix their drinks.

The Country was located in downtown Barstow. Anyone driving by would typically see chopped Harleys sitting out front. I was so comfortable there that I spent many of my off duty evenings there too, enjoying the clouds of cigarette smoke and the stench of exhaled booze mixed with perfumes and colognes.

On one such evening, I smiled and dropped the eight ball into the corner pocked and said, “Rack em up, boys. Tonight I can’t be beat.” The atmosphere was alive with partying marines and soldiers from local bases, as well as bikers and locals looking to get laid, drunk, score or sell speed (methamphetamine), or dance to the live music of a local band.

As the challenger racked the balls, I watched Dude, a customer about 30 years old with long hair and a Fu Manchu mustache, walk in the back door. “What’s happenin, Richard?” My nickname in Barstow, where I grew up, has been ‘Little Richard’ since junior high days. “How’s it goin’ Bro?” he asked before he sidled up and whispered into my ear, “Can you get me a quarter of speed?”

As the cue ball scattered the rack of balls, I turned around so my challenger couldn’t hear me and said, “Sorry, I don’t know anyone around here that has any right now.”

“Okay, I’ll check with ya later.”

I remember thinking while I started dropping more balls into the pockets: *Does he really expect me to stop what I’m doing and go on a search to get him a quarter? I wanna dance with Sherie—hopefully it’ll be a slow dance. I would really like to get into her pants. Look at her—that beautiful long blonde hair and those tan legs. Damn, I love summertime!* My challenger won the game, so I paid him five dollars and walked into the adjoining room.

“Make me a Monkey Brain, and make it snappy!” I said to the bartender

“Yes *Sir*!” Charles replied with an accommodating smile and a salute. “Is there anything else I can do for you this evening, *Sir*?”

“Yeah, hook me up with Sherie.”

“Get your own fucking dates,” he grumbled. “There’re plenty to choose from in here.”

Charles was around my age, tall, good looking with curly hair, and had recently been discharged from the Army. We became friends in the Country before either of us worked there. Unlike me, he was a snappy dresser with nice vests and seemed always to have on a new pair of Levis. He reminded me of the Fonz.

I don't remember how long Dude had been patronizing the bar, but I'd been serving him long enough that we called each other by name. Later that night he approached me again. Again I couldn't help him. *Damn! Sherie is looking good tonight. I like the way she looks at me when we're dancing. I'm gonna have to check out how she looks at other men while she's dancing with them. If she looks at others that way, then the task before me might be more challenging than it's worth.*

Two former *California Country* bartenders were also in the bar that night. About ten o'clock, one of them said, "Richard, Janis and I have some quarters for sale. We need to sell as much as possible tonight because we're leaving town tomorrow to make a new life for ourselves."

I sympathized with wanting to get out of town. Having spent so many of my younger years in Barstow, I remember thinking the same thing.

"Hey, if I'm gonna try to move some of this for you, I should know how good it is."

"Okay," he said, "let's go to the back room."

While he was getting a quarter out, I went to my stash place and retrieved my rig. "I hope you don't mind," I said, "but I wouldn't think of doing drugs any other way."

He plopped a quarter down and said, "I don't use needles but I don't care if you do."

While I was preparing my fix, I asked, "Why are you leaving Barstow?"

"I'm sick of this life, Richard. I'm sick of using speed, I'm sick of constantly looking for it. I'm sick of fighting with my old lady over it, and I'm sick of this suck-ass little town and all the dirty fucking, lying, thieving, backstabbing, scumbag speed freaks."

"Wow," I said as I inserted the needle into my arm. "You really are fed up."

While watching the blood flow into the syringe before I pushed down the plunger, he replied, "Yeah, Richard, I've never wanted to get away from anywhere this much in my entire life."

About an hour later, Dude approached me again. This time I acquired a quarter for him, but I was doing it more for the couple that was selling it, than for him. We made the transaction on the back steps, away from all the commotion in the bar.

The next day I was sitting at the bar having a drink when Dude walked in the back door. *Like me, he's probably coming in for a beer.* "Hey Richard, remember me?'

"Of course I do, Dude. How's it going?"

He flashed his badge and while taking his handcuffs out he said, "You are under arrest for sales of methamphetamine. You have the right to remain silent . . ."

As we were walking out to his undercover car, I said, "You fucking cops will go to any lengths to keep a fun-loving guy from having a good time, won't you?"

"I guess so, if you call dealing drugs fun."

"Dealing drugs? Bullshit! You nagged me until I scored it for you. I didn't even have to leave the bar to get it. That's not drug-dealing. I thought I was doing you a favor—good customer relations, you know."

"Yeah, yeah, I know. Who did you get it from, anyway?"

"Do you really expect me to tell you that?"

"Hey, it's your ass that's going to prison if you don't."

"Fuck you!"

I had experience with public defenders before, and this time was no different, so I retained another one. She was a young, fair-skinned black woman, very tall, fresh out of law school and out to save the world. She carried herself graciously, giving me the impression of an Indian goddess. The energy she put into my case really impressed me. She said I was clearly a victim of entrapment and politics. In my jury trial, she fought the case on the basis of entrapment. She fought her heart out, but her inexperience against a practiced deputy district attorney brought me a conviction.

Just my fucking luck—a clear case of entrapment and politics, and I was still convicted. The entire criminal justice system has been fucking with me for as long as I can remember. Why don't they go after child molesters and rapists? Why a fun-loving free spirit like me? I'd like to put a fucking bomb at the sheriff's station and blow those worthless, scumbag mother fuckers to hell where they belong. God damn, I hate 'em.

This attitude is typical of drug addicts. One would be lucky to find one addict out of a hundred who has an internal locus of control. Almost always, addicts place the blame outwards rather than being accountable.

I filed an appeal, of course, but that process takes a long time. As for the political implications, my public defender said that it was an election year, and that the county sheriff's department was doing a sweep in bars known for drug trafficking. This sweep was part of the incumbent sheriff's reelection campaign for his war on drugs. At the same time, the county needed to use up the fiscal year's funding provided by the state to hire extra duty vice officers so the following year's funding wouldn't be cut or diminished. Unfortunately, my attorney couldn't use any of these reasons as a defense.

The probation department recommended one year in the county jail and three years formal probation. I was aware that the judge went along with the recommendation of the probation department. I thought a year was preposterous, so I contested the probation department's recommendation and requested a hearing in hopes of getting the sentence modified. After I subpoenaed my mom and a couple other character witnesses, the hearing was moved 30 miles away to Victorville. Following the testimony of the witnesses, the judge rendered his decision:

"Mr. Smethers, after hearing all the testimony, it is my opinion that the recommendation of the county probation department is fair. However, I am willing to modify it. I will allow you to serve six months, with a six-month stay for six months." His ruling meant that, after serving six months, if I didn't get into any trouble whatever (no dirty urinalysis and no brushes with the law), for six months, he'd dismiss the other six months. The three-year probation stood. I was happy with the outcome. It was worth going through the process of a hearing. I asked the judge for a stay of execution to take care of personal matters and he granted it.

I had two weeks to party. I stayed wired on speed as much as possible, and when I only had about four days left, I managed to stay awake the entire time. I talked nonstop—24/7—for three days. I went to some friends' house and talked their ears off, and when I sensed they were getting annoyed with my incessant babble, I went to another tweaker's house and did the same thing. For several hours I went from house to house and did the same. On *the third day* without sleep, which was always my goal when using speed, my friend Crazy asked, "Richard, have you considered the possibility that you might be losing your mind?"

"I don't think so. I only have a few days left of freedom. If I start doing much thinking, I'm liable to get depressed. As it is, I'm having one hell of a good time. I'm not giving my mind a chance to start dwelling on something as depressing as going to jail for six months."

"Oh," replied Crazy, "I didn't think of it as a defense mechanism. That makes sense." One of the new friends I found while working at the California Country was Crazy. He and I knew each other by reputation from the sixties but we weren't personally acquainted back then. Because we had so many mutual friends from the past, we too became friends. One of the reasons I liked Crazy was because he was a dichotomy, in that he was affable, and at the same time crude, using a lot of street slang mixed with sparks of intelligence.

Few hard core speed addicts use the way I did. Most of them stay wired instead of coming down after a three or four day run. After awhile their bodies adapt, and they are able to eat and sleep and get erections. To do this, they buy large quantities and sell it so they can stay high. I didn't do that. I didn't have a car and I didn't have money to buy large quantities. I usually had to clean up for visits to probation officers (POs) or court appearances. The side effects are different with people who stay on it continuously, as opposed to people who come down for a few days before starting on another run. Whenever I started a run, I couldn't eat, sleep, or get erections. So, people who are always under the influence don't have a *third day* phenomenon.

The third day made me giddy, goofy, talkative, and witty. I remember thinking at the time, *if they could make a drug that made me feel like it was—the third day—all the time, I'd be hooked for life.* Of course, it didn't occur to me that I was probably already hooked for life anyway.

On the appointed day, I turned myself in and started my six-month sentence. It had been approximately 20 years since I'd served county time at Glen Helen Rehabilitation Center, better known as Camp Snoopy. Now I was much older, but Camp Snoopy hadn't changed much. I was placed in minimum security and landed a job cleaning dorms. I spent my time writing letters and making new friends and making plans for when I was to be released. My thinking was that m*ost of these fucking wimps in here talk a lot of shit about cleaning up when they get out. Shit, I don't have any ridiculous notions like that. I figure doing a* *little time periodically is like paying dues in order to live the way I want.* I expressed this attitude in a letter to my daughter (to whom I'll refer to later) while I was at Camp Snoopy:

> "Once I'm outta here, my probation officer (PO) will probably violate me, then I'll get put back in here until my new trial comes up [I was referring to my appeal]. I'm not being pessimistic, I'm being realistic. I was out from under Mom's apron strings a long time ago, so I'm not gonna leap when a PO says frog."

I don't remember much about that stint at Camp Snoopy, other than writing a lot of letters and just trying to get through each boring day. We had a motto: Another day, another quarter, another day shorter. We were paid a quarter a day for a full days work. Four months later (two months off for good behavior and work time), I was released, and my first thoughts were, *Now all I have to do is get rid of this bothersome probation. There's no way I can survive another probation in Barstow.* With that thought in mind, I approached my PO with a solution.

"McEcheron," I said, "I'm undoubtedly going back to jail if I stay in Barstow. This town is saturated with speed; even the cops use it. I need to get outta here, so I was hoping that you'd let me move back to Las Vegas."

After a short discussion, he said, "Okay John, here are some monthly reports. If you miss even once, you will be extradited back to Barstow on a probation violation, and this holds even if you're late. If I don't have that report in this office by the fifth of every month, you can count on another stretch in Glen Helen. Extradition over the state line isn't a problem because before you leave here you're gonna sign extradition papers. Do you agree?"

"I do, but don't you think you're being a little harsh by violating me for being a little late?

"Yes, it is harsh. Accept it or don't go."

Walking out of his office, I remember thinking, *Wow, I didn't think it'd be this easy. I thought I'd be appointed courtesy supervision in Vegas*, which meant that I'd have to establish residence there and then meet with the courtesy PO every month. Instead, all I had to do was go to Vegas once a month and drop a monthly report in a mailbox. So, I succeeded—I was rid of the probation. I screamed out with joy once I was outside the court house: *Now I can continue to drink and use without worrying about piss tests and being harassed by a fucking PO Fuck going back to Vegas—I'm having way too much fun here.*

Twice I went to Vegas, dropped a report in the mail, and then came right back. Having total freedom again I lived dangerously and continued using speed intravenously.

One day Crazy and I were visiting Cheryl, a pretty Native American woman. She had a loud and boisterous personality, which conflicted with her looks. I always got a kick out of watching her go off on guys in the Country when they'd try to pick her up. Later she became my girlfriend. After buying an eight-ball (an eighth of an ounce) of speed, the three of us were at Cheryl's trailer getting ready to fix when there was a knock on the door. Cheryl peeked out of the window and said, "Fuck, it's the cops! C'mon Crazy, let's go outside and talk to them while Richard stashes the shit." I went into the bathroom and injected a quarter gram as fast as I could. Then I hid the rest under the sink and walked into the living room from where I could hear them talking outside.

They were looking for Cheryl's husband who'd recently escaped from custody. Her husband was also on probation with McEcheron, who incidentally, was with the cop. Then I heard McEcheron's voice. "Is there anyone else in the trailer?"

Knowing they were going to search anyway, Cheryl said, "Yeah, Little Richard is in there."

McEcheron replied, "What? Little Richard as in John Smethers?"

"Yeah,"

The gig was up, so I walked out the door and into the loving arms of my PO. "So, living in Las Vegas, huh? Let me see your arms, *Little Richard*." Sure enough, he found fresh tracks. After relative freedom for over two months, I returned to Camp Snoopy to do the remaining six months of my sentence. Waiting in the Barstow jail for the bus to the county jail wasn't bad, but being in the county jail pending court or waiting for the bus to Camp Snoopy was always pure hell.

The county was rife with bullies who charged inexperienced inmates taxes, for protection. In fact, they targeted anyone who looked vulnerable to them. You could feel their eyes on you, constantly trying to figure out how and what they could get from you. For example, anyone wearing sneakers who wasn't capable of defending themselves would inevitably lose them, either by force or theft while sleeping. I always left my shoes in my property with the rest of my clothes and wore county issue along with the orange jumpsuit the county provided. I didn't buy much at commissary either, just the bare necessities. Buying a lot of candy and frivolous items was a clear message that an inmate had money on the books. It also helped to keep to yourself and not talk much. Be polite and respond when addressed, but that's it. Keep a low profile, and they can't learn much about you. That's what I did.

That wasn't the case, however, with one of the prisoners in the day room. Some guys don't know when to keep their mouths shut. This guy tried talking shit like he was a bad ass. Because of his mouth, an inmate beat him to a bloody pulp. Knowing the guards would be showing up soon, I started toward my cell along with some others. When I looked back, he was lying in a very large pool of blood. I never heard whether he lived or died.

Once I arrived at Camp Snoopy, I landed a job as a typist clerk. I typed TV schedules and the daily work sheets for work crews, and assigned bunks and jobs to the fish line (incoming inmates). These duties gave an inmate clerk quite a bit of power.

Inmates voted for the TV programs they wanted to watch. If the vote was close and inmates in one camp wanted to insure that their program was selected, I was the person who could make it happen. If an inmate wanted a day off, as long as I wasn't asked too often, I could simply not list his name on a work sheet. If an inmate wanted his homeboy assigned a bunk next to his, I could do that too.

I boasted about the power of my position in a letter to my daughter, which partly explains why I was rolled up and sent to discipline for what I thought was for no apparent reason. All mail is censored and I knew that, so why I thought I was being persecuted unfairly, I don't know. I'm sure they resented my boasting, but they evidently couldn't discipline me for that, so they blamed it on a letter I'd written to my friend, Lisa, who was doing time in prison. In the letter, I included a racist poem. When I was brought before the classification board, the board members said I was being disciplined for spreading racist propaganda and inciting a riot.

As it turned out, I spent nearly a year there, which turned out to be ten months after deducting time off for 'work time'. My 'good time' though was taken away because of the disciplinary action. Upon my release I went to see my PO and asked, "Hey McEcheron, is it okay if I move back to Las Vegas?"

He just looked at me, shook his head and said, "If I thought you were serious, I'd lock you up again right now."

We both laughed and then he made me pee into a bottle. I gave him dirty tests periodically, but he didn't want to revoke my probation and send me to prison. I was 43 years old and had never been to the joint. I believe he was convinced that I was making an effort to stay clean that time. McEcheron was a recovering alcoholic, so he had some insights that worked to my advantage. However, after my seventh dirty test, he violated my probation, but instead of recommending another jail sentence, he reinstated my probation, and I was appointed another PO. I think he liked me and didn't want to be the one to send me to prison.

When I went back to work at *The Country,* one of my steady customers offered me an old car that he didn't need anymore. After putting a battery and gas in it, I was back on the road again.

Roberson, my next PO, said, "John, I won't let you get seven dirty tests. If you start pulling that shit with me you're going to prison. I also strongly advise that you dissociate from Patsy. It isn't in your best interest to be involved with a woman with such a flagrant reputation for drug use and promiscuity." All the women I associated with used drugs and were promiscuous. *So what?* I thought.

"Probation officers," I said with scorn, "are control freaks. You even want to control where I put my dick. Do I also need permission to whack off?"

"Watch your mouth, John. I don't think you want me to take a dislike to you. I can make your life very uncomfortable."

"Yeah, I know. My mouth has often gotten me into trouble."

Patsy didn't last much longer anyway, but it had nothing to do with Roberson's scathing admonition. After my fifth dirty test, he kept his promise and revoked my probation. I went back to court on the original felony charge. Probation was a failure. I, however, had managed to stay out nine months this time.

Judge Leroy Simmons, who almost 20 years before was my Uncle Cecil's attorney for an armed robbery case, sentenced me to three years in the California Department of Corrections (CDC). He then gave me a stay of execution of two weeks to take care of personal matters.

I wasn't on probation anymore, so I had two weeks to get wild and crazy. I spent most of that time awake, reaching my *third day* twice. A favorite pastime for tweakers in Barstow was going to the dump and searching for treasures. The dump was where I preferred to be when experiencing my *third day.* It was amazing to me that so much valuable stuff could be found there. It was like being turned loose in Wal*Mart, except that it was outside and we'd dig through garbage, dirty baby diapers, discarded food, dead cows, and just about anything from a tin can to a rusted church organ. But it was really fun.

Most of my *third day* nighttime hours were spent at various dumpsites. While scavenging through the debris I'd talk to myself, sing to myself, articulate theories, fantasize about women, throw shit around, kick things, and laugh like my laughing apparatus was on a limited time schedule. I pictured people seeing me through some kind of television monitor, and that idea made me laugh even more. The *third day* made me feel completely uninhibited.

My friend and fellow bartender, Charles, and I were in the old car that the old man gave me, and we were on our way to the dump in Hinkley. Once we left the main road, I started driving on an ungraded part that was rife with obstructions such as big rocks, boards, and various objects that had fallen off trucks. We bounced up and down so violently that our heads kept hitting the roof. It felt like we were on some kind of amusement park ride. Finally I came to an abrupt stop, looked over at Charles and said, "Damn... I'm awake."

"What?"

"I thought I was asleep and dreaming this. That's why I didn't slow down. I figured since I was dreaming, I couldn't hurt this old car, so I kept driving like we and the car were invulnerable or something. I mean, you can't fuck up the car if you're dreaming, right?"

"Wow! How long have you been awake, Richard?"

His question was relative because normal people don't experience such bizarre head trips. Sleep deprivation often adds elements of psychopathology that aren't experienced while simply being under the influence. To me, however, what happened was phenomenal, and it was as fun as any amusement park ride would be. Though it was through sleep deprivation, I experienced a substance-induced psychotic episode, more commonly known as amphetamine psychosis.

"This is my *third day*, Charles. I wish I could stay just like this all the time and forever. This is what I live for."

"You're gonna be living in a mental institution if you get like this very often."

"So what? If I feel like this, I won't care where I'm at."

Charles just looked at me and said, "You're nuts."

At home, I turned what is now my study into what I then called my geek room. Speed freaks were often referred to as geeks or geekers. They were also referred to as tweakers, and many had an obsession for collecting junk. I had so much dump-junk in that little room that three people could barely fit in there at the same time. The junk went almost to the ceiling of each wall. I spent many hours in there listening to music, building lamps, and fiddling with all kinds of other electrical gadgets I'd found at the dump. About once a week I'd blow a fuse in my mom's house. That didn't really matter because I'd found plenty at the dump to replace them with. I found an antique cigarette lighter that I still have, but I also brought home a whole bunch of worthless junk like dice, fingernail clippers, marbles, and anything else that caught my fancy. Just about anything I acquired two of, I made a collection out of. That was not unusual behavior among dump tweakers.

When tweaking in my little room, I often talked to myself. *I wonder if I should shoot some more. No, I better not. I just did some an hour ago, and I don't have that much left. It's only midnight though. I'd rather stay up tonight and sleep tomorrow. No, shit, I'm getting tired.* I *better do some more. No... Yeah, fuck it. We only live once.*

~

I showed up in court at the appointed time, but I wasn't there to surrender. Judge Simmons asked, "Are you ready Mr. Smethers?"

"Your Honor, I'm hoping you'll give me two more weeks. My mom is here with me and she'd like to say something."

"Hello, Mrs. Smethers, I believe the last time I saw you was when I represented your brother."

"Yes it was. I've been in and out of the hospital recently, and I could really use him at home a little longer. I'm sure, unless there's other complications, that I'll have my strength back in two weeks."

"Okay, I'll expect you back here on the first of October, John."

"Thank you, sir."

I was back on the streets and shooting as much speed as I could get my hands on. I experienced my *third day* ecstasy a couple more times before D-day.

Again, the day arrived for me to surrender, but I wasn't prepared to go to prison yet. I took the chance that he'd give me another stay.

"Mr. Smethers, I assume you brought your toothbrush."

"Your Honor, my mom isn't recovering as fast as she expected. In fact, she wasn't even able to come down here today. I need two more weeks to watch over her. If you'll give me that, I promise that I'll make other arrangements for her if she isn't any better by then."

"You should have made those arrangements this time."

I said, "I know." I gave him the most pitiful look that I could muster, and then held my breath.

My mom was 73 years old and not in good health. The judge saw that with his own eyes at my previous appearance, so he granted me another two weeks.

I didn't have time to work, so I quit my job at *The* Country. I needed every waking hour to party it up—I didn't want to miss anything. During the previous year or two, I'd spent a lot of time in Grandview at my friend Leroy's house. He was a Viet Nam vet who loved telling stories about his experiences during the war. For a while I even lived with him; in fact, Crazy, who was also a Viet Nam vet, lived with him at the same time. Leroy always had meth.

I don't remember how I found out, maybe the newspaper, but probably through my friend Rogers (we pronounced his name in the plural) that I learned about Leroy's death. At the time, Rogers was Leroy's bodyguard. Leroy felt he needed one because of the high volume of drugs he was dealing in. Rogers, however, wasn't on the job one night when Leroy was murdered. He wasn't murdered by the type of people that Rogers was supposed to be protecting him from. Instead, it was a neighborhood teenager who was smitten with the woman Leroy was living with. Eventually the boy was exonerated and Leroy was vilified as a drug trafficking enemy of the people.

When the time came to surrender to Judge Simmons, I was there, but not to surrender. "Are you ready Mr. Smethers?" The Judge asked.

"Your Honor, have you heard about the murder a few days ago in Grandview?"

"Yes, I have."

"Leroy was a friend of the family. We've known the whole family for years. I graduated from high school with his sister, and I know his brother. Leroy and I were very close, and my mom and dad were fond of him. I know how many times you've granted me a stay, and I wouldn't be asking again if this terrible thing hadn't happened. I'd certainly appreciate it if you'd allow me to attend his funeral."

"Mr. Smethers, why do I have the feeling that I'm being taken down the garden path lane?"

"I can't say, your honor, but I hope that you believe me."

The good judge granted me another two-week stay; however, I had no intention of turning myself in when the time was up. They were just going to have to catch me. I consumed as much speed as I could. Everybody I knew was generous because they knew I was going to prison soon, so again I pushed myself to the limit. I reached my *third day* a couple more times. During the previous couple years, I needed to clean my system out periodically because of visits to probation officers. After taking a piss test, I could then hit the streets and strive for that *third day* buzz again.

Two or three weeks had passed since I was supposed to turn myself in. I figured my mom's house was being watched so I didn't go there, but I called her periodically. When the bartender did a last call for alcohol at the Country one night, I went to my old friend Jody's place. He and I tweaked together for three or four hours before I excused myself to get a couple hours sleep. I went out to my car and crashed on the front seat. A little after dawn, there was a tapping on my car window, and when I looked up, I saw Jody's mother standing there. I raised up and rolled down the window. "Richard, Jody's place is burning down and he tells me you're on the lam, so you better get outta here before the police get here."

"Thanks Doloros, I'll do that." I shook my head and then gazed at the 50-foot high flames for a couple minutes, which ended up being a couple minutes too long. I started the old Ford Falcon and started to leave. On my way out, I saw the Fire Marshall coming toward me. He stopped, stepped out of his car, and stopped me. He said, "You're gonna have to stay here. This fire is under investigation and we need to ask some questions."

I said, "Okay," then turned around and went back. I stood beside my car watching the flames again for awhile until a police car pulled up. *This is it*, I thought. I was scared shitless and I started thinking about what my first penitentiary experience was going to be like. *Oh shit! Back in that boring fucking Barstow jail for a week or so, then it's back to the fucking county again. God, I hate that place. Shit, here he comes.* Of course they found the warrant and I was arrested, plus they booked me for being under the influence. When I appeared in front of Judge Simmons again, he asked, "Why didn't you show up to surrender, Mr. Smethers?"

"Because I was scared, Your Honor. I've never been in prison before. I didn't abscond, I was still in the area. I just couldn't bring myself to surrender three years of my life. I knew that I'd get caught sooner or later."

He seemed to understand and dismissed both the failure to appear and the under the influence charges. I also pled guilty to my two pending DUI charges because I didn't want to be stuck in the county jail fighting them. I was given time served for both DUIs. That ruling meant that the time I was to serve for the felony also served for the two DUIs. That was a big break because I didn't have to pay fines, go to DUI school, or suffer the loss of my driver license. Judge Simmons then remanded me to CDC. By and large I was treated quite fairly but nobody could have convinced me of that then. Though my appeal dragged on for two more years, I eventually lost that too.

~

When they called my name and announced the title of my doctoral dissertation, I slowly walked up to the president of the institute to get my degree. When I returned to my seat, waiting for the rest of the students to receive theirs, I thought of my childhood and all the variables that could have predisposed me to so many years of drug and alcohol addiction.

CHAPTER TWO

Predispositions to Addiction

Because I was stoned for more than 30 years of my life, a good memory has eluded me. The best tool I have in reconstructing my past is my police record since there were so many arrests. My work history from the Social Security Administration was also helpful, but not to the extent that my police record was. Without these two documents, the events of my life would remain jumbled as to who, when, where, why, and what happened during my years of addiction. With so many arrests, my cases weren't resolved for months, because of multiple continuances, court or jury trials, or plea bargains. Even with this recorded guidance, it has been a challenge piecing the events of my life together.

In a way, I'm grateful for the lifestyle I led for so long. Baring my soul in these pages has worked to my advantage in the sense that I am seeking redemption and self-acceptance. I have to understand my life from a perspective of purpose. What was it all for? I also have to forgive myself for the pain I've caused my loved ones, especially my parents and my *numero uno*, my daughter Lynda, otherwise known as Snivels.

Out of my mom's five brothers and one sister, I was the closest to my uncle Orvil, who was a hard-core alcoholic for over 50 years. I was close to only two of about 15 cousins, so my family ties were limited to very few relatives. After my parents were married in 1939, they didn't expect to have a child. My mom was supposed to be incapable of childbirth. When she defied a medical prognosis, my birth made a marriage destined for divorce last for another 23 years, ending instead with the death of my father.

I was born on Monday, 22 January 1945, in Los Angeles, California in the Lincoln Heights Hospital on Soto Street. I was born the same year as the bomb, Hitler's suicide, and Mussolini's execution. It was also the same year that *The Lost Weekend* earned a best picture Oscar. The title characterizes most of my life. I even considered making the title of this book *The Lost Life,* because so much of my life is missing from my memory.

I had a happy childhood. When reflecting on *when* the seeds of drug and alcohol use and criminality were planted in my young mind, I am reminded of the time, when I was about eight years old, I picked a flower off someone's bush, and then noticed a police car coming around the corner. Immediately, I took off running. I ran up to my friend Arthur's door and banged on it. When he answered, I quickly went inside, turned around, looked down the street, then closed the door and said emphatically, "The cops are after me!" Something attracted me to a lifestyle characteristic of the behavior I was portraying. Did I really think the cops were after me? Probably not. Did I want my friend to think the cops were after me? I Probably did. During that time-period when my friends and I played good-guy/bad-guy, I always wanted to be the good guy. It's like I wanted to be a good bad-guy. This dichotomy has remained with me for most of my life. My grandma used to say that I had God in one eye and the devil in the other.

Whether it was from Sunday school or from my parents or both, I misconstrued God's punishment for bad behavior. My misconception came from the word "punish" which I interpreted as "punch." I had this image of a big fist reaching down from the sky and punching me in the stomach if I were bad. Early childhood development is replete with visual and psychological metaphors and similes. We forget most of them, but for some reason, I remember this one.

When I was about seven or eight, a schoolmate and I were riding our bikes around the neighborhood when he pointed to a car driving by and said, "See that guy in that car?

"Yeah."

"He's a drug addict."

Wow! A drug addict! I was enthralled. Every time I saw him driving around the L.A. suburb in which we lived, I'd watch until he was out of sight. *I wonder if he's hopped up right now? I wonder if he sticks needles in his arm? I wonder how many people he killed for dope*? Today I still wonder why I was so captivated with such a dark underworld figure. I also wonder how intrigued I would've been if I'd seen what is today rated as one of the worst movies of all time, a propaganda film made in the 1930s entitled *Reefer Madness*. Maybe I did see it, and that's what caused me to be so fascinated. Out of curiosity, I recently bought the DVD, and it definitely lives up to its reputation.

I was occasionally taken to visit cousins. The oldest, Sonny, had an edge that included lying, stealing and fighting. I'm convinced that he too contributed to my morbid fascination with antisocial behavior. Of course, professionals in the field of addictions point to the influence of family alcohol use, such as my mom's periodic alcoholism or my two uncles' hard-core alcoholism. Professionals in the field also talk about the evils of society as causes of drug addiction. They often mention overcrowded slums, the failure of cities to provide adequate recreation and educational facilities, the effects of racial or religious intolerance, the corruption or laxity of law enforcement, the lack of old-fashioned values and discipline in the home and so on. I cannot place the blame on any of those reasons. How can we know for sure what causes a person to become an addict?

I believe the causes are subtler, such as my morbid fascination with marginalized sectors of society; however, if I were forced to choose one single cause of addiction, I'd point to peer influence. I never knew anyone who became an addict all by himself or herself. Although alcohol is also a drug, alcoholism is different because it's legal. We see our parents, friends, and relatives indulging in alcoholic beverages, we see drinking in popular media, and we see it advertised. It's ubiquitous.

My maternal grandmother, the only grandparent I knew personally, was an integral part of my early childhood. I remember Grandma telling me that I was a distant relative of Jesse James. She was born in Fort Smith, Arkansas in 1889, so her early childhood memories were rife with legends of Jesse James as a folk hero. It's highly unlikely that my ancestry is adorned with such a legendary figure, but if it is, then perhaps I inherited my criminal proclivities naturally. Inside all of us run the streams of our ancestors, their good and bad qualities, and their gifts and liabilities. I loved my grandma, so if she was impressed with Jessie James, then I was too, procucing another subtle influence predisposing me to a dark side of life.

In the summer of 1954, my parents moved from East LA to Newberry, which is 20 miles east of Barstow, California. My dad asked if I would like to go to a military school for the summer while our new house was under construction. He made it sound exciting, and I would only be attending for the summer. Being caught up in a major life change, my parents probably didn't stop to consider that I was an only child between the fourth and fifth grade who'd never been away from home. They applied, and I was accepted into Mt. Lowe Military Academy in Altadena, California. I hated it. Marching, drilling, parade rest, attention, about face, lights out, taps, reveille. It was a veritable nightmare. I'd gotten into trouble for talking back to superior officers, for not eating all my food at meals, and even for marching out of step. I was always in trouble. Just for getting into my locker after lights out, I had to stand at parade rest for an entire day. I cried every night and I wrote letters every day begging to go home. I made promises that no kid on earth could keep—*Please, just get me outta here. I'll do anything you ask!*

My mom stayed with her sister in LA during the construction of our new house, but I wanted to be around all the action, so *finally*, after getting out of military school, I went to Newberry. There were tents set up for sleeping quarters and we cooked outside. Orvil and Red, my two drunken uncles, were also there, and I saw the down side of their alcoholism daily. I especially remember them being passed out in one of the tents with empty wine bottles scattered all around, with what seemed like thousands of flies buzzing around their heads like Orvil and Red were dead animals. The stench from not bathing, mixed with the foul odor of flatulence and alcohol was disgusting. Flies were crawling up their noses, on their lips, and into their mouths. It was a gross sight. The average person might think that a memory like that would discourage alcohol use later on. Our unconscious minds, however, are influenced by good and bad alike, so it isn't that remarkable that I'd be influenced in such a way.

We moved into our new home later that summer. Newberry was a hellhole that my mom and I both hated. Today it's called Newberry Springs, and it's gone from bad to worse and back again. For years it was a haven for the production of methamphetamine, and for the tweakers who used it. I understand it's not as bad anymore. I can't help thinking of my two years in Newberry when I see the athel trees that are so common to the high desert. They surrounded our house and were spread around the immediate property.

In Newberry, I hung out with a future thug named Richard. I learned about sex from him. There was a shed on the school grounds where we'd go to talk. "Johnny," he said as he sat down on a bench with tools scattered all over it, "have you ever done it to a girl?"

"No, have you?"

Richard smiled coyly and said, "Yeah, I do the wild thing with my sister all the time."

"What's it like?"

"Really neat, man. Wouldn't you like to try it?"

"I guess."

I was interested, and I couldn't really relate because I'd never even had an erection—I was simply too young. Anyway, following his lead, the next day we took one of our classmates to the shed.

As he reclaimed his spot on the tool bench, Richard asked, "Barbara, would you like to join up with us?"

"What do you mean?"

"Johnny and I are starting a club and we thought you might like to join us."

"Okay," she said, seemingly pleased that she was being asked.

"Well, you'll have to be initiated first before you can be a member."

"What's that mean?"

"Well, uh, you have to let us do it to you."

"Do what?"

"You know, what grown-ups do to make babies."

"Oh... Well, uh, let me think about it and I'll tell you tomorrow."

The next day when we walked into the classroom, the principal called Richard and me into his office, and there sat Barbara with her parents. We were severely spanked, and then expelled. A week later, however, I was reinstated, but Richard wasn't. After considering all the circumstances, the principal came to the realization that this proposition was something that Richard instigated, using me to help him get something that he wanted. Still, there was a morbid interest on my part or I wouldn't have gone along with Richard's proposition, even though I knew we were doing something wrong. On the other hand, my dad used to tell me that friends too easily influenced me, and with my present hindsight I realize that he was right.

I was at Richard's house a week or two later when this conversation took place: "Johnny, since they won't let me back into school, we're moving away."

"Where to?"

"Westminster," he said, "wherever that is."

"We could write letters," I suggested.

"Hey yeah, and if I get offered any dope, I'll let you know in a letter. And if you get offered any, you can tell me in a letter."

Prior to this, I'd told him about the drug addict in my neighborhood in LA, and we agreed that we'd both like to try dope if we ever had the chance. Richard was also fascinated with dope addicts.

"Okay, but don't write about dope in the letter," I said. "Instead, we'll put a skull and crossbones at the bottom of the page just in case our parents read it first. I'll know then that you found some. I'll do the same if I find any. Maybe we could talk our parents into taking us for a visit or something." Was this another, rather formidable, early-childhood influence predisposing me to drug experimentation?

Another influence was the rebellious nature of rock and roll, which started in 1954, the year that we moved to Newberry. On each side of our house there was room to park a car, but my parents parked on the west side. Somehow I found out that radio reception was better on the east side, so I'd often pull the car over there and listen to KPOP (kaypop) in Los Angeles, a radio station that played all the new music that Alan Freed coined as rock-n-roll. It was then that I started my record collection, first 78s and then 45s. Movies of the era such as *Rock Around the Clock, Blackboard Jungle, High School Confidential, Rebel Without a Cause*, many of which incorporated rock-n-roll in the soundtracks, were also influential.

Another incident happened just before we moved into Barstow. I will preface this story by explaining that my parents taught me to drive on those lonely desert roads in Newberry when I was only nine years old, so by the time I was eleven I was a relatively experienced driver. My only handicap was my size. I was always short for my age, so when driving I'd look *under* the steering wheel to see where I was going. One day my mom let me drive on the main highway, which at the time was Route 66. There were no freeways yet. We were pulled over by a highway patrolman because he couldn't see anybody driving the car. I was written up a for driving without a license, and my mom received one for permitting an unlicensed driver to drive. That was my first traffic citation, and I was proud of it. My seventh grade school year started before our court date, and I remember bragging in the school locker room that I'd gotten a ticket. I showed it off like a badge of honor. I tell this story because it's just another, however minor, unconscious machination toward personifying a figure with the edge that I was attracted to.

By the time we moved to Barstow in the summer of 1956, my dad had a security patrol service that he renamed Barstow Merchants Patrol, so named because he protected the buildings of local merchants. He was paid a monthly fee to check their businesses twice before and twice after midnight.

Because my dad patrolled the Barstow Theater, I had free show privileges, and before long I met other boys my age. Some lived in the neighborhood that we moved into, some I knew from going to the show on Friday nights, and others I knew in school, of course. I am still friends with a few of these guys today. It was in the seventh grade when I was tagged with the name Little Richard, which would stay with me for the next 35 years. Sometimes, I am still addressed as Richard; therefore, in the following pages my name will alternately be John, Johnny, Richard, or Little Richard.

It was also in the seventh grade that I met my first future ex-wife, Lynda. She was one of the most beautiful girls in the school. Still being too young to be *sexually* attracted, I was mesmerized by her facial beauty. Lynda had the face of an angel. We became friends and later we made out in my bedroom while listening to records. Then the unthinkable happened—she became the girlfriend of one of my friends and they went steady for a couple of years. When they broke up permanently, she started dating older guys, so my feelings were hurt again. Lynda was two years older than me, so what she was doing was natural, but then I was incapable of understanding why she was attracted to older guys.

Then another unthinkable happened. Her parents turned her in to the authorities as an incorrigible. She went from juvenile hall to a foster home, back home, and then back and forth between juvenile hall and other foster homes, and finally to the Ventura School for Girls,where she met her first future ex-husband, who was in the Los Diablos motorcycle gang. She later had three kids by him.

We'd kept in touch during her stays in various foster homes. I loved getting those perfumed letters. I was also fascinated with the experiences she was having in juvenile hall, foster homes, and the school for girls. Unknowingly, even sweet Lynda was contributing predispositional influences. (For more on the causes and conditions of addiction and recovery, read my book, *Scumbag Sewer Rats: An Archetypal Understanding of Criminalized Drug Addicts*.)

~

Once the commencement was over, and I said my goodbyes to my former classmates, my daughter, her husband, my two grandkids, and I climbed into their car for the trip home. After some conversation regarding my graduation, I closed my eyes and thought about my early teen years.

CHAPTER THREE

The Fifties

Decades don't historically and sociologically conform to even numbers. The way I see it, the fifties didn't start until the advent of Rock and Roll, which is generally considered to be 1954. I went into junior high school in the summer of '56 when I was eleven years old. My drinking started the following year. It was a Friday night thing before football games, school dances, and double features at the Barstow Theater. At that age we needed to find someone old enough to buy beer, wine or liquor for us. One night the older brother of my friend, Ricky, got us a half-pint of gin each, and then Butch, Ricky, and I went to a secluded spot to drink it.

"Hey, Butch, don't drink it fast. You'll get too fucked up."

"Isn't that the point?"

"You're right," I said. "Mint-flavored or not, it still tastes bad."

"Okay guys," said Ricky, "don't ask me to pick you up when you fall on your asses."

After staggering around the bleachers of the football game and visiting with friends, we walked to the local hangout called the Burger Haven to socialize. Standing outside with my back to the squad car that had just entered the driveway, my condition must have been obvious to the police officer. Being 50 years ago and drunk on mint gin, I can only speculate as to the dialogue that went on between the officer and me. It probably went something like this:

"John, I think you better come with me before you get into trouble."

"Fuck you!"

That's when I did the only thing that I distinctly remember. I took a swing at him. I was undoubtedly showing off in front of my friends. For some reason he didn't take me to jail. I am assuming that he took me home because there were no legal repercussions for my behavior. The next morning, however, my parents made me clean up the vomit on the front porch, in the bathroom, and in my bedroom. The entire house reeked. To this day, if I were to smell mint gin, I'm sure I'd gag.

On another occasion, my friends and I went to a school dance after drinking a bottle of wine each. Feeling six feet tall and bullet proof, I ventured over to ask the cheerleader, Dorothea, to dance. I know I wouldn't have asked her unless I was drunk. As we were dancing, I felt gas building up, so I decided to let it out quietly, and then dance away from the smell so someone else would get the blame. Something unexpected happened. It wasn't gas. It was the wine squirts. Immediately, I excused myself and went outside to decide what to do. I didn't want to go home, so my only option was to go behind the classrooms, take my pants off, wipe my butt with my underwear, throw them away, and then put my pants back on and return as though nothing happened. However, I didn't have the balls to ask Dorothea to dance again.

These demoralizing incidents are characteristic of alcoholics, especially with budding ones, but not demoralizing enough to make them not drink anymore. No, the lives of those addicted to chemical substances are fraught with experiences, that are, more often than not, forgotten about.

Odors have a way of bringing back memories. I remember the smell of popcorn and our forays into the forbidden cry room at the old Barstow Theater to smoke cigarettes or sneak drinks out of a half pint bottle.

Sometimes my friends and I would ditch school and get drunk. If we couldn't get anyone over 21 to buy beer for us, we stole it out of markets along with various food items. Then we'd go up to B Hill or to someone's house whose parents weren't home and drink it. During this time I ran with Gimmy. We called him that because after drinking all *his* beer, he'd want some of ours. He'd say, "C'mon man, gimmy a drink." For money, sometimes Gimmy and I would steal empty pop bottles and sell them. We'd also go into shops downtown and snatch muscular dystrophy donation jars and then run like hell. We needed to supplement our allowance money from our parents to support our growing dependency on alcohol. Of course, we explained it away as just needing more money to have fun with.

It was during these junior high school years that my parents became the legal guardians of my friend Dennis. He was homeless at the time, living in Gimmy's garage. Because I was an only child, my parents thought that he'd be good company for their often bored and lonely boy. They liked Dennis, so they went through the legal procedure to become his legal guardians.

Dennis added lucrative elements to Gimmy's and my bag of tricks. He introduced us to *hitting cars*—breaking into and robbing them for anything we thought was of any value. We weren't old enough to have fences for expensive items so we mainly looked for money or objects we could use or sell or simply throw away.

There were about four of us who took turns *borrowing* our parents' cars at night while they were sleeping. Although my other friends and I were doing this before Dennis showed up, he was accused of being the instigator because of his rebellious nature. Eventually my parents asked Dennis to leave. He was with us less than a year but he showed up again later in my life.

About a year after Dennis left, my dad found me a job as a dishwasher. Uncle Neal's Pancake House was also where the bus station was housed and I worked my butt off there. Anytime I hear the old song "Mule Skinner Blues," I can't help thinking of the old crippled man I worked beside at Uncle Neal's. The old man didn't have any teeth so it was difficult to understand him. Weekly paychecks enabled me to make bigger deposits to my back account than I'd previously deposited with money earned from punch cards, deposit on bottles, and cash from birthday and Christmas gifts. When a couple of my friends bought Cushman Eagle Motor Scooters for their paper routes, I wanted one too, even though I didn't have a paper route. Somehow I managed to talk my dad into letting me spend my bank account money on a brand-new Cushman.

During the summer of that year, the red light bandit, Caryl Chessman, was executed, the shower scene in *Psycho* were the talk of the country, and I was starting to climb the lower rungs of the alcoholic ladder. I was jailed three times that year, all within a five-month period, none of which would've occurred had I not been drinking. The first arrest was for curfew violation.

Feeling both down and angry that I was put behind bars for such a trivial offense, I started wondering what I could do to show my hostility. About an hour after I'd been placed in the juvenile cell, two more juveniles joined me. This was the first time I became personally acquainted with Huck and his friend Jim. Still one of my best friends today, Huck and I hit it off right away in that old jail cell. We'd all been drinking, and what was at first a depressive and a potentially explosive situation, turned into more fun than any of us would've had if we hadn't been locked up. We climbed up and down the bars like monkeys, tore up the mattresses, had wet toilet paper fights, stuffed toilet paper into the hole in the floor—plugging it up as well as the toilet—and because the juvenile cell door was entered directly from the outside, we yelled obscenities to the officers walking around outside. The old jail had a particular odor, and I still smell it sometimes when I go into a rest room at a public park. It's probably something to do with what they use to clean floors and walls with. Anyway, after that, jail wasn't much of a threat to me.

About a year later, like Dennis before him, Huck was homeless. Again, my parents became the legal guardians of another wayward boy. Huck wasn't the bad influence that Dennis was, and like Dennis he stayed only for a year or so. When Huck was 16, he got a girl pregnant and was married. They had a little boy, whom he named John Robert, after me and our friend Bobby, whose nickname was Hickey. During that time Hickey, Huck, Gimmy, and I became known as the big four.

Not long after being jailed for the curfew violation, Gimmy and I were jailed for petty theft, and before the summer was over, I landed in jail for my first DUI on my Cushman Eagle. Each time I was released to the custody of my parents.

It's not difficult to understand why my parents were starting to regret the way I spent my bank account money. They weren't strict disciplinarians, though there were times when I accused them of being so. Being put on restriction was how I was punished once I entered junior high school. Prior to that, however, my dad made me get a switch from a tree. When he eventually drew blood on my back, my mom put a stop to it, threatening to turn him in to the authorities if he did it again. He didn't do it again and switches became a thing of the past. Rather than continue brooding over my wretched situation when I was in jail for the DUI, I chose to ponder more cheerful memories.

I pictured Lynda's sweet face. She was the one who hurt my feelings by going out with older guys when I was younger. She was out of foster homes and living with her mother in Chino, California. Lynda's mother worked at the women's prison there. I thought about the road trip that Hickey and I took on my scooter to visit her. Her mother was strict so we didn't get to visit very long. After a glorious visit with my dream girl, we trekked back to Barstow on my Cushman. Thinking of Lynda was a respite I could enjoy when my life was at its worst.

As a result of my first DUI, my driver's license was revoked before I was eligible to get it. At that time instruction permits (or learner's permits) were issued by the DMV to those who'd reached 15 years of age, providing they'd successfully completed a driver-training course. With an instruction permit, the holder could legally drive a car as long as a licensed driver accompanied them, and they could also operate a motor scooter. I was also placed on formal probation for one year—the first of five formal probations I'd be placed on in my life, not to mention the summary or informal probations that were generally given for lesser offenses. Realizing what a horrible mistake the Cushman Eagle was, my dad sold it.

~

As with any budding alcoholic, my condition progressed, but later it had to share my affection with other chemical substances. Had I started using illicit drugs prior to graduating high school, I would not have graduated. It's a wonder that I did anyway, and even more of a wonder that I graduated on time with the rest of my class. Because of my drinking and partying priorities, every year I received Ds and Fs, then I'd make up the Fs in summer school to keep from being held back.

Around Christmas that year, my dad had aluminum siding put on our house. At the same time he hired the contractor to convert the garage into a large bedroom with an additional room and a bathroom. My parents told me that the construction was a combination Christmas and birthday present. Getting one present for both Christmas and my birthday always annoyed me. My birthday is in January, almost a month after Christmas, therefore I wasn't very grateful. I wasn't capable of realizing how little I deserved any gifts, considering all the trouble I'd gotten into in the recent past, but like most teenagers, I was self-centered and unappreciative. I couldn't have asked for better parents, but I didn't realize it. I came to *expect* their generosity.

It was the year Paul Newman played *The Hustler*. Nineteen sixty-one was also the year of the Bay of Pigs and the death of Ernest Hemingway. I was 16 years old. I'll always remember Hickey driving his low-rider '53 Chevy and singing *Runaway* along with Del Shannon on the radio. It was his favorite song. It was also the year for me to get laid for the first time. "Hey, let's go to Ash Meadows and get some pussy," Hickey suggested.

"I'm game," I said, trying not to act too excited.

"We can get a sixer each and by the time we get there we'll have a buzz."

From Barstow it was 60 miles to Baker on old highway 91, eighty miles on highway 127 to Death Valley Junction, and seven miles on a dirt road to Ash Meadows. It was a big ranch. There was an airstrip for small aircraft, a motel, and a bar, but we went straight to the whorehouse—a building off to the side with a big bright red light on it. Hickey and I hadn't been there before, but our friend Ray Lay had, so he'd explained to us what it was going to be like. We called him Ray Lay because he was horny all the time, and L-e-y were the first three letters of his last name.

"C'mon in, boys, and by all means enjoy yourselves," said the big fat smiling madam who answered the door.

We walked in acting as cool as possible. Hickey and I sat down while Ray Lay dropped a quarter into the jukebox. He played *Runaway*. Hickey smiled and said, "I don't care what people say about you Ray, you're all right in my book."

At about the same time that I was noticing the plush carpet and the expensive pictures on the wall, five young women walked out in bikinis and lined up in front of us. I wasn't expecting them to be so beautiful. With my heart pounding, I thought, *wow, I must have died and gone to heaven. I actually get to get naked with one of them and do what I think about all the time. Damn, look at that one!* Then Ray Lay stood up and took the best looking one by the hand and started walking back through a long hallway. *Shit! I shoulda done that*! Taking Ray's lead, Hickey and I stood up at the same time. Fortunately we didn't go for the same girl. As we walked hand in hand down the hall, the pretty blonde squeezed my hand, smiled and said, "Hi, my name is Linda."

"I'm John," I said, preferring not to use my nickname of Little Richard. I thought it ironic that her name was Linda. I couldn't help thinking of my Lynda. We walked into a small room with a single bed and then she asked, "What would you like?"

I said, "What can I get?"

"Ten dollars for a straight lay. Twenty dollars for a half and half, and..."

I cut her off and asked, "What's a half and half?"

"A blowjob and a lay."

"I want that," I said taking in the aroma of the room that smelled like she'd just taken a bath.

I gave her a twenty-dollar bill and she said, "Take off your clothes and I'll be right back."

She was beautiful, and she made my first experience a memorable one. I especially remember her putting water in small pan when we were finished, and then asking me to stand up. When I did, she placed the pan under my genitals. I took that as a cue to wash myself. I started to do that, but she stopped me. After a chuckle, she said "No, I'll do that for you, honey."

"Oh," I said, feeling embarrassed.

On the way back home I said, "Linda, the one I had, said that out of all the men she'd had in there, I was the best."

"Little Richard," replied Ray, "they get paid to say that."

"Did the one you had say that to you?" Asked Hickey.

"No, but she said my dick was bigger than any man she'd ever been with."

Before I could tell Ray that they get paid to say that, Hickey turned on the dome light, reached into his shirt pocket, held up a piece of paper, smiled and said, "I bet they don't give their phone number and home address to every man that comes in there."

"If you believe she really lives at that address, then you're dumber than I thought you were," said Ray.

"I thought of that," Hickey quipped, "and I asked her if she really expected me to believe she was giving me her real address. Then she showed me her driver's license."

"Ha!" I laughed, "are you going to take her home to meet your parents?"

Bobby's low-rider Chevy is an ever-present image in my memory of those good ole days, but an even more memorable image is that of my first car. While I was on probation for the DUI on my scooter, I was spending money fixing up my 58 Chevy. After a year with a revoked license, I finally went down and took the tests. I'd been driving since I was nine so the driving test was a breeze. After studying the handbook, I passed the written test as well. I was finally back on the road. Right away, I had it lowered. For the times, it was a sharp looking car.

During this time, I started hanging around with Dirty Dick. He was a friend of my best friend Hickey. One night, Dirty Dick, another guy, and I were out drinking in my 58 Chevy. After we took the other guy home, Dirty Dick and I bought more beer and went to our favorite drinking spot. While drinking and smoking pot I asked, "Hey, Dirty Dick, think you'll ever try shooting heroin?"

"Fuck no!" he said with a disgusted look on his face, "Shooting heroin to me is as repulsive as fucking my mother." Ironically, three years later he was a heroin addict. After we caught a buzz, we left to go somewhere. Back in town, I jumped a curb and hit a brick wall. I tried to back out but I couldn't because the bumper was pushed into the flat tire. Sizing the situation up immediately, Dirty Dick said, "Fuck, Johnny, we can't just sit here and wait for the cops. We're too fucked up."

"Let's go get your car and just leave mine here." With that said, we ran to my house, which was just around the corner. We got into Dirty Dick's 57 Chevy and went back to our drinking spot to talk about what just happened. After popping another beer I said, "Wonder what's gonna happen now?"

"One thing is for sure," said Dirty Dick, "staying there would've landed us both in jail."

"I might land in jail anyway."

"Yeah, but it won't be for drunk driving."

"That's true," I said as finished my beer and lit a cigarette.

When I went home that night I told my mom what happened. My dad owned and operated a security business, and he was out on patrol, so I didn't have to worry about him for the time being. A short time after I went to bed, the police knocked on the door. When they asked my mom if they could talk to me, she told them I wasn't home. She didn't realize that she was enabling me to continue my behavior. The car was towed and a week later I received a citation in the mail for reckless driving and leaving the scene of an accident, which was, like Dirty Dick said, a hell of a lot better than another DUI. By then I had fine payments to make, so the car payments to my parents were losing priority. Fortunately, I was covered by my dad's insurance, so after getting it fixed, I was back on the road again. The insurance company wouldn't insure me any longer on his policy, so I was required to get an assigned-risk policy on my own. *Fuck that, I'll drive anyway*, I thought. It wasn't long before I wrecked my car again.

My friends convinced me that I could still drive it if I took off the fender, so I borrowed my dad's toolbox and took it off. *God damn, what an eyesore! I wonder if girls will still go out with me? Damn, I better ask Sandy out before she sees it.*

Sandy was a Barstow High School cheerleader and drop-dead gorgeous. She worked in the box office at the Barstow Theater. I don't know how she managed to sell tickets when she was so busy waving at all the guys honking at her as they drove by. We knew each other pretty well from having so many classes together in school, so I built up some courage and gave her a call.

It was after dark when I picked Sandy up from work, but instead of parking my car in front of the theater where my missing fender would be visible, I parked down the street a ways in the shadows. I left the motor running because there was a chance it wouldn't start. Once she was in my car, I had to show off and drive up and down main street a couple times so everybody could see Sandy sitting next to me. Then we went to the A & W for a soda. I unconsciously turned off the motor. *Oh shit*, I thought, *after driving up and down Main Street with the lights on it's probably not gonna start.*

It didn't. I was embarrassed. I managed to get a jump, but I beat myself up pretty bad for being such a show off. The sweetheart of a girl that she was, Sandy acted like it didn't bother her. She even accepted another date with me. Instead of total humiliation, I was on cloud nine again with anticipation.

I didn't want to take another chance driving my car, so Sandy and I double dated with Bob and Carol. The four of us went to the drive-in theater. I respected Sandy, so I'm sure I didn't try to get very far; besides Bob and Carol were in the front seat. Shy as I was with girls then, I'm sure I was happy enough just making out with her. I hadn't turned into an unconscionable leg-humping horn dog that I would become later.

It was time for another road trip, and what better road trip could there be than one to Ash Meadows where I could feed my Sandy-frustrated libido? Gimmy and I and two other guys loaded up an ice chest with beer and headed out. This time I had the experience of having been there before, so after the girls lined up, I immediately grabbed the best looking one and waved good-bye to my friends as she and I walked down the hallway. The looks on the guys' faces reminded me of the way I'd felt when Ray Lay did the same thing.

After doing the wild thing with the girls, we started back, taking turns bragging about our sexual feats with the whores. Hanz said, "the one I had said she never saw a man with a dick as big as mine."

"Hanz," I said, "they get paid to say that."

By the time we were halfway to Baker everybody was passed out. Then I passed out. Bear in mind that highway 127 between Death Valley Junction and Baker was (and still is) a dark and lonely road with very little traffic. How I managed to pass out when one of the only cars on the road that night was right in front of me, I don't know, but I sideswiped the on-coming car. The collision woke everybody up.

We made it all the way home without getting caught, and the only damage to my car was the smashed molding that was left after the previous collision. After that, my friend Dirty Dick started calling me Johnny the Crasher. He and my friends started making statements like, "Yeah, Little Richard can't help himself, he likes hearing the sound of metal against metal."

~

Returning home from my graduation commencement, I sat down in my chair and recalled what I said to the woman who interviewed me as a candidate for the doctoral program at Pacifica. I told her that once I earned my Ph.D., I planned on writing a memoir. With that in mind, I went into my study and started this book with the following chapter about my prison experience.

CHAPTER FOUR

Lower Education

In November 89', after a couple weeks in the county jail, I caught the bus to what was then called the Chino Guiding Center. It's called a reception center now. All the trouble I'd gotten into from chapter one, and the two DUIs I had pending, finally caught up with me. The first cell blocks I was placed in brought home the reality that I was really in prison. The cell was on the third tier of the west yard. It looked to me like the oldest cellblock there. I visualized my Uncle Cecil being in this very cell 50 years previous. That cell was only temporary, however, and before long I was transferred to the west yard where I stayed for a couple weeks.

Wow, this looks neat! I thought on my first day on the west yard. The sun was shining, and there was a cool breeze. The playground was full with inmates playing soccer, some basketball, and others throwing Frisbees. Some were working out on a weight pile, playing cards on picnic tables, and the tennis and handball courts were also occupied. Others in the bleachers cheered their favorite team while watching a softball game, and many were just walking around the yard. Ironically, I couldn't find anyone who looked unhappy or depressed.

In 1989, inmates in the California Department of Corrections (CDC), were well provided for, having little, if no responsibility for themselves. Our clothes and linen were cleaned every week—all we had to do was drop it off and pick it up when it was ready. Our meals were provided—all we had to do was show up, wait in line, and eat. We didn't even have to clean up after ourselves. There was a big yard to play in and a weight pile where many inmates could flex their muscles, show off, and be macho before strutting around the yard acting tough, much like kids do on a playground. There were also those who built reputations, status and respect from their peers by controlling the drug and alcohol flow, managing moneymaking schemes, and having their subordinates do their dirty work. Drugs were plentiful on the yard, and pruno (home made wine) was easily made. Every three months inmates could have money and material things (a package) sent to them from the outside. If they were married, they could spend a weekend in a bungalow with their wives and relieve themselves sexually. In maximum-security prisons that have cells, inmates could enjoy watching their own color TV sets. The state even provided free rolling tobacco. Most prison facilities had hobby crafts, and there were jobs by which money (though not very much) could be earned. Some of what I just mentioned isn't valid today. The weight piles, free tobacco, packages from home, and televisions in the cells are all gone.

In Chino, I hung out with three tweakers from Barstow. Frank had a store, which means he was the connection for whatever anyone needed. Upon my arrival, he gave me a welcome package with all the amenities needed for personal hygiene, plus other articles. I was fortunate to have him as my friend.

While walking the yard one day, I asked a man doing three years for burglary, "Say Rip Off, do you really want to get out? I get the impression that you like it here."

"Nah, I don't like it here, Homes, I can't wait to hit the streets, but while I'm here, I'm making the best of it."

Rip Off believed what he said. However, many inmates like Rip Off have an unconscious want and/or need to stay where they are, where they don't have to be responsible. When inmates like him are released, they usually don't make a single attempt to reform their lives. They continue committing crimes and using drugs with no worry of getting caught. Why worry? Getting caught means some judge will just send them back home where their peers will welcome them back with open arms.

I can't count the times I was in the county jail and heard conversations, such as the following one I had with Jinx, a three-time loser and a barrel of a man with an earring and multiple tats: "Have you gone to court yet, bro?"

"Tomorrow, homeboy, then it's back to the joint," said Jinx as though his mind was at ease.

"Sounds like you want to go there."

"Shit Homes, I'd rather do a year in the joint than thirty days in this hole."

That is a typical attitude of ex-cons in the county jail awaiting sentencing, and I agree, for county jail is hell compared to the day-care center environment of many prison systems.

Recidivism is high. The typical inmate will be back in the joint on a violation or with a new beef usually within months after release-day, then the revolving door process continues. My friend Dirty Dick, a lifer heroin addict, is a good example. He spent approximately 20 years in prison before he received his three 25-to-life sentences. He'll be 125 years old before he's eligible for parole.

Consciously, many ex-cons *believe* they don't want to get caught, but unconsciously their behavior is saying: "I really don't care if I get caught or not." So, how do people on the inside prepare for a law-abiding life on the outside? They usually don't. being relieved of responsibility by being placed in the prison system, inmates become less responsible. Their self-reliance is atrophied, and there is no rehabilitation. Here's a conversation I had with one of my bunkies in Chino: "What are you going to do when you get out, Sagus?"

"Get high, dude, first thing."

"Aren't you afraid of getting violated and sent back?"

"Nah, it's okay to wait a couple days before you report to a PO."

Sagus didn't *plan* on returning to prison on a violation, but with his dope-fiend mentality, he didn't stand a chance of being successfully discharged from parole.

One afternoon I was standing in line for commissary when I witnessed this conversation:

Toe-tag said, "You know, I wouldn't be here for robbin that liquor store if the fucking clutch wasn't bad in my old Chevy. Just as I was taking off, the motor died. I started it, and then it died again. That happened three fucking times, homes. By the time I made it to the corner, there was red lights everywhere."

"I hear ya bro. If my ole lady's mom wouldn't have turned me in, I wouldn't be here either," replied Straight Razor.

I understood those middle-aged bikers because I have often placed the blame for *my* behavior outside of *me*. It would have been a waste of time for me to say, "Toe-tag, you wouldn't be here for robbing that liquor store if you hadn't been robbing that liquor store." It's strange, but to them that obvious statement would've been absurd, and it would've been to me too, at that time, that is. Before I went to prison, my querulous old friend Dirty Dick called me on the phone to explain—or whine (most drug addicts are chronic whiners) about being arrested for a burglary he didn't commit. He said, "Johnny, can you believe it? The motherfuckers busted me for a burglary that I didn't do."

"Bummer, man. You should be able to beat it, though," I sympathized.

"Fuck, Johnny, I shouldn't have to beat the damn thing, I didn't do it. They shouldn't have arrested me in the first place."

He carried on for five minutes about the injustice of being wrongly accused. Finally, when he stopped talking long enough, I asked, "Why are you so outraged about this?"

"Johnny, I didn't do it! God damn them! The bastards are trying to frame me."

"Hey Dirty Dick."

"What?"

I calmly asked, "What about all those burglaries you didn't get caught for over the last twenty years?"

"What? Don't get carried away, Johnny. The fact is, I didn't fucking do it. This charge doesn't have anything to do with what I did before." He dismissed my question as being ridiculous.

This attitude is the same one I had concerning my case. I was also enraged: *The fucking bastards entrapped me. It was not my fault. The worthless scumbags were fucking with me. I was a victim of politics*. The truth is, if I hadn't sold drugs to undercover agents, I wouldn't have gone to prison for selling drugs. However, like Dirty Dick, I wasn't capable of being accountable for my actions.

Jointsters (a term I coined in my first book, *Scumbag Sewer Rats*, referring to criminalized drug addicts) don't think like normal people. They can justify anything. I used to say that my crimes were victimless because I didn't hurt anyone but myself by getting arrested for substance-related offenses. I would've had an automated response if someone had asked about the harm I was doing my family, the harm I could do while driving under the influence, or the harm I was doing to employers by ripping them off (hell, they could afford it). My daughter once said, "When he made my dad, God wasn't thinking straight."

The streets can be a frightening and depressing place for jointsters, because being responsible and accountable for their actions is foreign to them. An extreme and pathetic example is in the movie, *The Shawshank Redemption*, in which actor James Whitmore's character kills himself after being forced onto the streets against his will. If we have no opportunity to be responsible inside the walls, why should we become responsible outside of them?

As I walked around the yard, I could see the comfort zones that most of the inmates were in—they were relaxed and seemed at home. Their jovial camaraderie, "Hey, home-boy, what it be like? Gimmy five," would give anyone the impression that they were in their element. The human condition can get used to anything, and getting used to prison is all too visible there. When I see these types of jointsters on the street, most of them do *not* have the appearance of being in a comfort zone—that relaxed, at-home look. They seem to be more on edge, more serious. For good reason, they have much more to be serious and on edge about. Everything isn't handed to them the way it is in the joint. Thus, the archetype of the *puer aeternus* somewhat diminishes through prison indoctrination as the criminalized drug addict starts personifying the trickster archetype.

Consider this scenario from the streets: Zip, a tweaker, was attracted to Slam's wife, and when Slam was out of the room, Zip took the opportunity to look down her blouse. Slam's wife said, "Do you see something you like?"

Surprised by her boldness, Zip admitted that he did.

She said, "Well, is it worth $500?"

After thinking about it for about a millisecond, Zip said yes. She told him to be at her house around two p.m. Friday.

Zip showed up on time, paid the $500, did the wild thing with Slam's wife, then hurried away.

As usual, Slam came home from work at six p.m. and upon entering the house he asked his wife: "Hey, did Zip come by the house this afternoon?"

With a lump in her throat, she answered, "Uh... yes, he did."

Her heart skipped a beat when he asked: "And did he give you $500?"

After mustering up her best poker face, she replied: "Yeah, it's in the cookie jar, honey."

Slam, with a satisfied look on his face, said, "Good, Zip came by the work site this morning and borrowed $500. He promised to stop by here on his way home and leave the money with you." This is classic dope-fiend behavior—a real scumbag, right?

I'd been knocking on the door of the state penitentiary for many years. Chapter one describes what led me to prison and why I was finally admitted. At Jamestown, I was housed in a large gym that was packed with three-tiered bunks. Overcrowding in CDC was the order of the day (and still is) and tempers were short. I often found myself bored, so one day I went on a book search. I approached a hard-nosed looking guard and asked, "Sir, do you know where I might find a book to read?"

He turned around, glared at me and said, "Do I look like a fuckin librarian to you?"

"Hey!" I replied emphatically.

He jerked his head back around and gave me a stern look and said just as emphatically, "What?"

I calmly said, "It doesn't cost a thing to be nice."

The big brute started to say something, then stopped himself and turned away. He turned back again and started to say something else and stopped himself again. Looking as though he didn't know what the hell to do, he suddenly softened with a sigh and said, "You're right. You didn't ask for the way I spoke to you."Apologetically, he said that he didn't know where I could find a book. The inmates aren't the only ones who become hardened by prison life.

On the bus ride from Chino, I was seated next to a man about my age. Rick had been through the prison system before, so after befriending him I had a guide who could explain about the prison environment and some of the processes we'd be going through.

Sierra Conservation Center at Jamestown, California is where inmates are trained for fire camp. Fire camps are the lowest security facilities in CDC, which is just about no security at all—no gun towers, no firearms, and only one guard. Since I ended up at Sierra, I was hoping to go to a fire camp but that didn't happen. When I arrived at Jamestown I was placed on the level three yard.

Level one is minimum security with dorms that are left unlocked, enabling inmates to visit other dorms. Level two is still minimum security but not as much so as level one. The dorms are kept locked and guards come around every half-hour to let inmates in and out. To get back in, we'd have to show our prison I.D., which our housing number was on. At this level, inmates couldn't visit other dorms. Level three is medium security. At Jamestown, level three inmates have concrete, two-man cells with a big day room in the center. Levels four, five, and six are the highest levels of maximum security, which is how a prison is usually depicted in movies—with barred cells on multiple tiers, etc. At Jamestown, however, there were only levels one through three.

CDC has a point system that determines what security-level inmates are placed in. If an inmate has from zero to 18 points, he is placed on a level one yard, 19 to 27 points is level two; 28 to 37 is level three, and so forth, on up to level six. For every year that an inmate is sentenced to, he's given four points. For each of his previous county jail sentences, two points. If he's never been married, two points. If he's under 25 years of age, two points. If he didn't graduate from high school, two points. Never been in the military, two points.

More points are added for previous prison sentences, plus more for histories of escape. Specific charges such as arson, violence, and sex offenses also get additional points. If an inmate, however, was employed for at least six months prior to prison, then two points are deducted. With various other criteria, such as college degrees and various professions, additional points are deducted. I was sentenced to three years—12 points; I served three county jail sentences (excluding the ones preceding my prison sentence because they were for the case I was in prison for)—six points; having never been in the military—two points. A total of 20 points—level two. My description of the point system may not be exact, but I believe it's close.

When I arrived at Jamestown I was placed on the level three yard. It was new, with part of it still under construction. I was placed in level three when my points designated level two because of a shortage of bed space. Sometimes the prison administration is unable to adhere to its own system. I was in a two-man cell with another inmate. He was a speed freak and easy to get along with, so we talked a lot about our common drug experiences with meth. Many inmates actually prefer the living conditions of level three over lower levels because of the luxury of having a room to themselves. After two weeks on level three, I was transferred to level two. The next day when I went out on the yard, I found an environment similar to Chino, with the yard being full of activity—a virtual playground. This is where I hooked up with Rick again. Though Rick and I were assigned to different dorms, we still saw each other on the yard every day.

As soon as I walked into the dorm that I was assigned to, one of the inmates looked at me and said, "Look guys, they've sent Charley Manson to our dorm. I knew I looked rather shabby, but it didn't occur to me that I might look as menacing as Manson. From that time on my dorm-mates called me Manson.

Not having been assigned a job yet because of overcrowding, I started writing a novel. I used Rick as one of the main characters. Every day after writing a segment, Rick and I met on the yard and I'd read to him what I'd written. He *appeared to be* interested, but I believe he was just being nice because I made him one of the characters. After I was released, I changed that character's name to Hickey.

I finally landed a clerical job in the yard office, which is where I procured my prison mug shot. I hadn't worked there for very long before I saw a flyer that read "Project Change: Substance Abuse Education." It was a nine-week education and therapy program designed for pre-release inmates. On the flyer was a request for interviews. I knew that I'd never terminate parole successfully unless I refrained from drug and alcohol use, so I filled out the request form and interviewed for a place in the program. I only wanted to remain abstinent for as long as my parole lasted. After that I planned on returning to life as I knew it before I was incarcerated.

Once, when I was tending bar at The Country, one of my friends came in and ordered a soda. "What's up with this, Jerry?"

"I'm on parole. If I don't give my PO any dirty tests or have any brushes with the law, I'll get off parole early." Jerry and Lisa both were off parole 13 months after their releases, so I was determined to do the same.

I was accepted into Project Change six months prior to my release date. Since the program was just starting, they needed to fill the dorm that was allocated for the program. Later, only pre-release inmates in their last 60 days were eligible. I also managed to get a clerical position with Project Change. Never having used a computer, I found an inmate in the education department who tutored me until I was familiar enough with the word processing program on CDC's Apple computers, to type questionnaires, work sheets, and other educational material, much of it gleaned from Hazeldon recovery books. We held classes five days a week in the TV room of our dorm, and another part of the dorm was converted for other classroom activities. Whereas other dorms housed over 40 inmates, there were only 22 in ours because of Project Change.

Another reason I volunteered for the program was for the fringe benefits. Project Change students went to chow first and would be first in line for commissary and linen as well as mail call. Because he was an alcoholic, I explained all of this to Rick and encouraged him to volunteer too. He applied and was accepted. His heart wasn't in it though, but mine was by the time he came in. I could tell he was just going through the motions, and that he'd return to drinking when he hit the streets. Most alcoholics and drug addicts eventually do. Unfortunately, deep down in my psyche, I wasn't really very confident that I'd be able to stay clean either.

The letters I was receiving from my daughter, Snivels, even prior to my enrollment in Project Change, were motivational and rife with AA cliches and jargon. She seemed genuinely happy in sobriety. I was not much of a father to her and even less of a son to my mother. I caused them more anguish than I could ever hope to make up for. However, once I started digesting all the literature I was reading, and started taking a sincere interest in the Project Change program and everything the teachers were offering, I started feeling the guilt associated with addiction/recovery. I found myself seriously considering a life without drugs and alcohol, rather than just a temporary abstinence until I terminated parole. I seemed to really want it, not so much for me as for my family. After Snivels started reading my letters, which was now rife with 12-step cliches and jargon, her return letters were so full of hope, encouragement, and happiness that I became that much more determined to stay clean. She and my mom were so proud of me that I absolutely could not let them down after everything I'd put them through. Here is a letter I received from Snivels at that time.

Dear Dad,

Hey, hey, whad'ya know, a letter from your dear 'ole daughter! Miracles happen! How ya been? Me? Never been better! I'm working the 12 steps in every area of my life & now my reality is a better place to be. I'm unlearning old patters and recreating my life. It works!

I work at Bobs Big Boy now, and I'm paying back Grandma's money and saving for a car,... a Fiero. A used one of course, but I want a Fiero & it's already mine, I just have to claim it. So, by the time you get out, I'd love to take the drive to come and pick you up. I may come visit you if I get it sooner. We'll see what happens.

You know I haven't seen you in a long time. I'm dying to meet you again! Now that you're clean and sober, I get to meet 'you.' Not some crazy, party animal legend, but good ole John Smethers, father of mine. And you get to meet 'me.' Not a rebellious fuck-the-world, let's party, crazy adolescent, but good ole Lynda Smethers, daughter of yours. What an adventure this is gonna be!

Grandma reads 'Just for Today' every day so far. She heals every time she reads it. With the both of us doing good for ourselves, heals her. It's love. The better we get, the better she gets because then she's not a failure anymore. See what I mean? Guess I'm taking her inventory.

I think there's something you should know. You have raised a wonderful, beautiful, daughter who is successful! And do you know why? Because you are beautiful and wonderful and successful today! That's the truth.

I was thinking about my childhood and upbringing. And it was awesome! It was very exciting and sometimes dangerous. Perfect for me. Out of all the insane people and situations, I was taught how to survive. I can remember how you understood me when I needed a curling iron and bought me one. How you allowed me to go hang out with the black family down the street when you were prejudiced. How you allowed me to go to church with the neighbors and be baptized when you were atheist. How you took me to the movies on my 1st date with a Filipino boy whom you were prejudiced against. How you took me to dances with friends, and when you took me to buy clothes. No matter what crazy things we did and what happened you always let me be me. As my only parent, you tried to understand. Nobody could have told me about my period and about sex better than you did! You're the best mother I could ever have! I want to thank-you for the freedom of choice & belief you gave me, and for allowing me to create myself. If I had to be born again & choose my parents, I'd choose you! You did it perfectly! As for the harsh words and violent moments we exchanged, they are forgiven. For myself & you, we make a great team when we're clean and sober. I love you, I really do.

Your Baby Girl, Snivels

The asthma attacks were upon me again. One night I was so congested that I could hardly breathe, and I started to panic. I waved a white flag out of the dorm window, a signal of distress, until a guard showed up, unlocked the door, and escorted me to the infirmary. The attending nurse let me take a hit off of an inhaler. It didn't help, and she could tell, so against protocol, she allowed me to take another hit. She could tell that I was still in distress. She said that she wasn't authorized to give me an injection, so I'd have to wait until she could track down the doctor. Because there were three yards at Jamestown, the doctor could be on either one of them. She finally found him on the level three yard and he authorized a shot of Adrenalin.

I immediately felt relief. As the nurse was taking my temperature and blood pressure and filling out the paperwork, she asked, "How badly do you wheeze when you have these attacks?"

"I don't wheeze at all."

"Well," she said, "people with asthma wheeze."

"I don't wheeze. I just can't breathe. It's like I'm trying to breathe through a pinhole. This time it was so bad I was afraid that the pinhole would close."

"You probably don't have asthma. Be sure to sign up for sick call on your way back to the dorm. I think the doctor should examine you."

The next morning when everyone in the dorm was awake and starting their day, I drew their attention by holding up my can of Bugler and yelling, "Who wants this can of tobacco? I quit!"

There were jeers and taunts such as, "Sure you have, I'll give you three hours," or "You keep it, we don't want you bumming off of us."

"I'll tell you what," I yelled, "I'll start sucking dicks before I'll start smoking cigarettes again!" That statement opened a can of worms. My dorm mates raised their eyebrows and offered me cigarettes whenever they passed by my bunk. They'd follow me into the bathroom at night to see if I was smoking, and they'd lay traps for me, like leaving cigarettes on my bunk or slipping a pack into my shirt pocket. Prison isn't a very good place to make such statements so I really put my foot in my mouth, but I knew what I was doing. After making that statement, I had a major incentive not to start smoking again. I didn't and I still don't smoke to this day.

When I saw the doctor the next morning, he asked, "What made you think you have asthma?"

"They told me that in Chino when I got a physical." I lied actually. Dr. Woodyard in Barstow told me it was asthma, but I wanted to blame it on CDC.

The doctor said my problem was C.O.P.D., which is **c**hronic **o**bstruction **p**ulmonary **d**isease, caused from smoking. He said, "It can only get worse with every cigarette you smoke, so I strongly suggest that you quit."

I said, "I already have. I gave my tobacco away this morning." Then I told him what I said to the inmates in my dorm. He thought that was funny and was impressed with my strategy.

"If I don't smoke another cigarette," I asked, "how long will it take before my condition goes away?" He started shaking his head and replied, "Never. The damage is done. The good news is, it won't get any worse unless you start smoking." The doctor was wrong. It did go away about two years later. Evidently, CDC really did mis-diagnose me. I still don't know what I had.

~

In Project Change we were taught that we had a disease that was chronic, progressive, and fatal: chronic because it never went away, progressive because it kept getting worse, and fatal because it killed people on a regular basis. Today, however, I don't subscribe to the disease concept, and I explain why in my book *Scumbag Sewer Rats*. In Project Change we also learned about family dynamics such as co-dependency, about the addictive personality, barriers to intimacy, anger management, and a special focus on relapse prevention. We also did role playing in preparation for saying no. We covered a lot of the material that I encountered later as an intern at McAlister Institute in San Diego.

Project Change worked for me. Within four months I believed that I'd recovered from a seemingly hopeless case of mind and body. I was certain that I'd never drink or use again. The fact is, however, that even among those who are certain they will not drink or use anymore, most of them will sooner or later. The recovery rate is very low, and so it was with me.

Kathy, one of the teachers in the program, recognized my academic potential and suggested that I go to school when I was released. I said something like, 'Yeah, yeah, sounds like a good idea," but I wasn't serious and she could tell. She approached me on the matter several times, practically nagging. Finally, I started giving it some serious thought. I knew I'd be living with my mom when I was released. She was on her last legs, and I wanted to take care of her for as long as she had left. I figured that by going to school, I'd keep myself busy with homework when I was at home and could be of help to her, while doing something for myself. When Kathy heard me talking this way, she started believing I might be serious.

In Project Change, we watched a series of videos entitled *Breaking Barriers*. Gordon Graham, the presenter, elucidated the fact that if lasting change is going to take place, one has to monitor and discipline his thought processes; therefore, if I were going to stay clean and sober when I was released, I needed to change my thinking. As it was, almost every waking moment was spent thinking about either The California Country, how much fun the dump was, the people whom I drank and used, and the women I slept with. I came to realize that being in a recovery oriented environment and having this type of stinking thinking (12 step cliché) at the same time, was like slapping your wife and saying you love her at the same time. I asked myself, *how can intrinsic recovery take place with such a barrage of conflicting thoughts*?

All the great leaders throughout history have taught the principle that our lives are the result of our thoughts. Buddha said, "A man's life is the direct result of his thoughts." Solomon said, "As a man thinks in his heart so is he." Happiness comes from happy thoughts. Success comes from successful thoughts, failure from failing thoughts. So it is, that our thinking controls our lives.

Our minds have two parts: a conscious part and an unconscious part. The 'depth' component of depth psychology is the unconscious part. The conscious part is what we think and reason with, but the unconscious part controls bodily functions such as breathing, blood circulation, and digestion. It never sleeps and is working all the time. It's like a computer. It takes in data and processes it. It has a memory of everything that has ever happened to us, from the day we were born to the present moment. It is non-judgmental. It doesn't know what is good or what is bad. It doesn't care whether the thoughts come from us or from others. If we don't take the effort to program it positively, our unconscious will take direction from other people or from the environment or from our own self-talk.

I used to wonder why I didn't always get what I wanted or why I couldn't accomplish much. Perhaps I was sending negative messages to my unconscious, or maybe it picked up negative inputs from those around me. My dad said that I was too heavily influenced by my friends. He was right, I was. I have come to realize that if I am not happy in my own skin, then I have probably set up not being happy myself. I read somewhere that "if we are experiencing lack, we may have been thinking mostly in terms of shortage. If we wish to change, we must start thinking in terms of abundance and prosperity."

One of the tenets of Project Change was, if our lives are not what we want, we have the power to change. And we change by changing our thoughts, which are programmed to our unconscious.

Therefore, I invented a method to change my thinking: I decided to shoo my old thoughts away, and replace them with different thoughts. I did this quite literally. With my hand in a swishing motion by my ear, I shooed the recurring thoughts away and started thinking other thoughts. Walking around the prison yard shooing thoughts away in that manner, I could tell by the looks I was getting that I was being viewed through jaundiced eyes. *A nut case, I'm sure*, they must've thought. I didn't care. I was on the road to a new life without drugs and alcohol.

At first it took me a long time to remember to shoo the recurring thoughts away, so I only shooed them away two or three times a day. As time passed, however, I started shooing them away more often, and then even more often, until I was doing it a lot—maybe 20 or 30 or even 40 times a day. That's when I was getting so many of *the looks* from other inmates. After awhile I discovered that I wasn't shooing away thoughts as often. My thoughts started going back the other way. As time went on I shooed thoughts away less and less because I wasn't thinking the old thoughts as often anymore. I'd replaced them with new thoughts. And then... guess what? After about three or four months, I'd exorcized all those old thoughts by replacing them with thoughts of what I *really* wanted to be doing and where I *really* wanted to be when I was released. I visualized myself in NA meetings, and I visualized myself in Barstow College classrooms. I also visualized spending time at home taking care of my mom, which of course, served as further impetus to remain clean and sober. How could I be a comfort to my mother at the end of her life if I were still drinking and using drugs? Eventually, staying clean became the very most important thing in my life, even more important than my daughter and mother. Without total abstinence, what good would I have been to them? They may have been my incentive for *getting* clean, but *staying* clean finally became my top priority.

Rick couldn't hang with the program so he moved out. We still saw each other on the yard and we remained friends. I made other friends too, one of them being my bunky, Soledad. I continued my novel while I was in the program, and Soledad became interested in it, so I changed the name of one of the other characters to Soledad's given name. Every day he'd read what I'd written, but unlike Rick, Soledad made suggestions and comments. He was genuinely interested, but Rick, I came to realize, was just being polite. By that time I'd completed two grammar courses to improve my writing skills.

Rick, however, was a talented artist. He earned money by doing artwork on envelopes. He did a really nice one for me that I sent to Snivels, which she still has today. Rick also picked up debris off the ground such as little sticks, pieces of tin foil, stones, and bits of shrubbery. With this material, he made some awesome lifelike three-dimensional pictures, and he started spending more and more time in the hobby craft building. My favorite piece that Rick made, was a man on a chopped Harley driving down the road with the head of a buck dear hanging over his saddlebag. Above it read, A Country Boy Can Survive.

With my release date approaching, I tried to talk him out of that piece of artwork, but he wouldn't part with it. He said it was his favorite too. About a week after I was released, I received a package from Jamestown. To this day, that piece of artwork hangs in my gym. When people are in jail or prison together, they often make promises to keep in touch and hook up after they're released, but those promises are seldom kept. Rick was one of those who promised, and so were Soledad and another man. I gave them my phone number and address, but I never heard from any of them. So it was with me—I never contacted them either.

The prison scenarios we see in popular media are not the daily routine in most prisons, especially minimum-security yards. Wholesale boredom was the norm. I was on the yard one day, however, when I heard shots fired. I looked around and noticed that everybody on the yard was lying on the ground, so I did the same. Nobody told me that we were supposed to do that. When violence breaks out on the yard, a shot is fired from a gun tower. Then everyone's required to lie down until a voice on a loudspeaker releases us. That only happened once while I was there. Lock-downs, however, were quite frequent. For example, if there were tension between the races or between gang affiliations or between any groups, the entire prison population was kept locked in their dorms or cells. I experienced two lock-downs, but they were only for a couple weeks. Overall, prison lock-downs can and do last much longer than that.

A couple months before my release date, Kathy volunteered to help me with the tedious financial aide paperwork so I could get the federal Pell Grant when I was released. She also suggested that I send a letter to Barstow College and request a catalog. I received the catalog and when I received the financial aide paperwork, she helped me like she promised. I was 45 years old and was going to be a college student again. I tried twice when Barstow College was at the high school in the early sixties, and I tried again later at Long Beach City College. Both attempts were failures, so I came to believe that I wasn't college material. I am certain now that I wasn't—then.

Snivels started her recovery while I was in Camp Snoopy, before I went to prison. She still has letters I wrote to her during that time, plus the ones I wrote from Jamestown. After reading them, I am amazed at all the fatherly advice I was giving her. Some of it was actually sound, but most of it was from a refractory and hedonistic scumbag with an inflated male ego. One thing was consistent in those letters, however. I never failed to tell her how proud I was of her and how much I loved her. If nothing else, she grew up knowing she was loved.

Letters she wrote to me at Camp Snoopy and Jamestown were recovery oriented, and she mentioned several of my dope-fiend friends who were showing up in AA meetings. It was comforting to know that I was going to have friends at meetings when I was released, but because I considered myself more of a drug addict than an alcoholic (I never thought of alcohol as a drug), I planned on attending NA meetings. I eventually resolved to attend both. I knew that my old friend Huck and his wife Debbie helped found the NA program in Barstow, so I figured I'd be spending more time with them than with the alcoholics. It didn't turn out that way. I liked AA meetings better at the time. I knew more people there, plus the Alano Club (AA meeting house) was in walking distance from my mom's house. Ironically, I now like NA meetings better than the AA ones. It's really just a matter of taste and the types of people who attend. Some people don't like meetings at all where they live, so they travel to other towns for meetings.

As I approached my release date, I couldn't help notice how much weight I'd put on. When I arrived at Jamestown, I had a 30-inch waist. By the time I left it was 34. I wasn't yet familiar with the term "cardiovascular" but I intuited that walking or running would lose more pounds than lifting weights, so I started fast-walking around the yard. By the time I was out of prison, I dropped a few pounds, but I needed to continue exercising to drop more. I've been exercising consistently since, but getting weight *off* is so much more difficult than I thought it was going to be, and a hell of a lot easier to put back on.

As it turned out I was, and still am, grateful that I went to prison. I only served 13 months, having been given credit for the two six-month sentences I served at Camp Snoopy. I only spent 21 months altogether for that sales charge, but the most meaningful part was Project Change. There I was provided with all the building blocks for living a long and productive life free of drugs and alcohol. However, I still had a lesson or two to learn about how to accomplish that.

CHAPTER FIVE

A Growing Dependence

Having been released from prison and supposedly recovered from a hopeless case of mind and body, I joined Snivels and a few friends in meetings. But what did I recover from? It isn't just addiction to a substance that addicts need to recover from, it's also the addiction to a lifestyle and a way of thinking.

After graduating high school in 1962, my friend Big Head, with whom I'd been friends with since junior high, bought a chopper. His mother told him that if he bought a motorcycle he'd have to move out of her house. He bought a motorcycle and he moved out of her house. Again my parents came to the rescue. He didn't live with us very long, but to this day, I think my parents repeated taking in my friends because of the isolation I experienced as an only child. Friends often visited and spent the night during my junior high and high school years. My parents even tolerated our drinking in their home, believing that we were better off drinking there than on the streets. Parental behavior such as this is still prevalent today.

Without going into all the details of more than 40 arrests over a period of 30 years, I've included a copy of my criminal record at the back of this book. What's obvious is the connection to drugs and alcohol. Charges that aren't connected to drugs directly are connected indirectly in some way.

I loved my parents, but I sometimes wonder how I could've done much of what I did after they'd been so consistently good to me. One of the events that earned me "scumbag" status early on, for example, occurred while my parents were sleeping. One night I sneaked their car out and went out drinking and smoking pot with my friends. We went to the spot we'd dubbed The Canyon. Driving up the old canyon road, I ran over a big rock or up the side of a hill or something, and the car went over on its side. The damage wasn't all that bad, so we pushed it back onto its wheels. Amazingly, it started up, so we did what we went there to do. When we finished our beer, I took them home and returned the car to its parking space.

As I mentioned earlier, my mom was a periodic alcoholic, and on this particular weekend she'd been tying one on with her brother, Orvil. The next morning my dad came into my room and asked, "What happened to the Corvair?"

"What do you mean?" I replied innocently.

"Well, it looks like it was tipped over on its side."

As if I didn't know what he was talking about, I said, "I don't know, let's see." We walked outside and looked it over. After looking at it, I kind of shook my head and said, "Dad," and then motioning toward the house with my head, I said, "she's been drinking all weekend. Maybe you should ask her."

I don't know what transpired between them, and my dad never mentioned the incident again, but several years later I asked my mom about it. She said that she told him she couldn't remember damaging the car, but that it was possible. I believe that's what she told him, but probably in such a defiant way that further conversation about the incident would've been fruitless and ugly. The bottom line was that she managed to cover my ass without admitting to anything. I was under the impression that my dad couldn't be sure which of us did it, so he treated us both indifferently for a while. Eventually he forgot about it. Needless to say, my mother really loved me, and she went on proving it in many ways for the rest of her life, especially when it came to protecting me.

What I did was despicable. Why would I do that to my mother? How did I live with myself afterwards without the least bit of remorse? And why do so many parents put up with such reprehensible behavior?

To begin with, I didn't do the bad things I did *to* my mother. I was defending myself. My age and my growing defiance and self-centeredness enhanced by my growing dependence on chemical substances, made me very egocentric. As heartless as it may seem, rather than being remorseful, I thought I was being hip, slick, and cool by getting away with something, and for many years that was my *modus operandi*: getting away with something, pulling a fast one, getting over, tricking someone, pulling the wool over, a con job. This type of behavior is characteristic of a trickster, which I'll discuss later. It is also one of the premises of my previous book *Scumbag Sewer Rats.*

~

The fifties didn't end until '63, the year after I graduated from high school and the year that Marilyn Monroe died. The British Invasion in that year earmarked the beginning of an era. At least that's the way it I see it. Most of what happed in the sixties are remembered for what happened after '62. Most of the events between '59 and '63 had the ambiance of the fifties. There was still a fifties sound to Rock and Roll. The dance craze The Twist came out in 1960 and West Side Story in '61. In 1962 Earl Chandler's "*The Duke of Earl,*" which was reminiscent of the '50s do-wop music, was popular. One of my favorite songs of the era was "*Mockingbird*" by Inez and Charlie Foxx. Though the United States started sending troops to Viet Nam in the fifties, the Viet Nam War is thought of as a sixties event because the heavy fighting didn't start until 1965, and then the Tet Offensive in '68. The hippie movement, the Martin Luther King and Kennedy assassinations, student rebellions, and the Civil Rights movement all mark the sixties.

I don't remember the circumstances surrounding my arrest, but in October of 1963, I was sentenced to three days in the city jail for a probation violation. Again, I met new people, and again incarceration wasn't an unpleasant experience. For me, jail was not a deterrent to drug use, driving drunk, or drug-related criminal activity.

One winter, I worked with a guy named Jim in a fast-food restaurant. He introduced me to his friend James and the three of us went out drinking periodically. It was during this time that I received a letter from Lynda, my childhood sweetheart, who was living in Colton, CA. I didn't have a car at the time, but James did, so I talked him and Jim into taking me to see her. We loaded up his car with beer and hit the freeway.

This was the day that Kennedy was assassinated. Normal radio programming was interrupted with the coverage. As I reached over and turned off the radio, I said, “Damn, can’t they play a song once in a while? I’m getting sick and fucking tired of hearing about it.”

“No shit,” said James, “it’s not like they’re saying anything different. No matter what station you go to, there it is, bla bla bla.”

Lynda and her husband, Don, were living with her sister, Barbara. We were all sitting on the grass outside the house when Lynda took me inside and proudly showed me her infant son—the first of three she’d have with Don. We then returned to the front yard.

About fifteen minutes later, Barbara stuck her head out of the front door and said, “Lynda honey, you better come in now. I don’t want Don coming home from work while your friends are here.”

“Okay, Barb.” Lynda walked us out to the car and laid a wet one on me. I didn’t wash my lips for a month, it seems. I was in love with her and had been since we were kids in junior high school.

By 1964, I’d been through, maybe a dozen girlfriends, but the main focus in my life became drugs: sex and rock and roll became subordinate to my chemical indulgences. My old friend Goat turned me on to pot right after high school, and it became my drug of choice. I even preferred it over alcohol, but bennies (Benzedrine—later referred to as whites or cross-tops), reds (Seconal), and codeine cough syrup were substitutes that were rising in priority and sometimes taken concomitantly. Of course booze, being legal, was always an option if nothing else was available.

In May of ‘64, when I was 19 years old, Hickey, Denny, and I each bought a half-pint of vodka and some orange juice and drank it before we went to a party in Grandview. About eleven o’clock Hickey and Denny wanted to leave, but my friends Hamburger and Dirty Dick wouldn’t let me go with them, so I stayed. I actually wanted to go home with Hickey and Denny, so when Hamburger and Dirty Dick weren’t looking, I caught a ride home with someone else. When leaving Grandview, we came upon a site that I’ll never forget for as long as I live: Denny’s overturned car and an ambulance with blinking red lights. Drunk and emotionally distraught, I jumped out of the car and started babbling and running after the ambulance as it pulled away. My ride picked me up down the road and we went to the hospital. When we arrived, I saw Denny as he was being rolled into the hospital on a gurney, but I didn’t see Hickey.

The next morning I went to work, but I was an emotional wreck, still upset and worried about the condition of my best friend. My coworker, Larry, tried to console me: "Don't worry, Little Richard, he'll pull through."

"They'd shipped Hickey to Berdoo because Barstow Hospital wasn't equipped to handle his condition. "I just hope he made it there in time, Larry," I said as my voice cracked.

"He'll be okay, I'm sure of it."

The telephone rang. "Jr. Bun Boy, John speaking."

"Hi honey," my mom said, "I don't know how to tell you this except to say that I have bad news."

"What?" I said, holding my breath.

"I'm sorry honey, but Bobby didn't make it."

I heard my mom tell my dad, "He's crying."

I was devastated. When I hung up the phone, I just stood there. *Oh no,* I started choking up and my eyes started getting blurry from the tears welling up. *I don't have a best friend anymore.* Like a zombie, I walked to the front where Larry was working. When he looked at me, I said softly, "He's dead."

Larry crossed himself and said, "I'm really sorry Little Richard." Nobody close to me had died before except my grandmother, but I wasn't really that close to her. Hickey's parents let me organize the funeral the way I wanted. Of course I consulted with them on various matters for their approval. I suggested putting Hickey's picture on his headstone and they did. I wanted to choose the pallbearers and they let me. I also helped with flower arrangements and other formalities. As if I weren't already developing a chronic dependency on drugs and alcohol, I used Hickey's death to justify what I considered a temporary overindulgence. *I've never felt like this before. It's all I think about. Fuck, I don't know what to do, I can't get it out of my mind.*

It was several years before the dreams started. From then on I had recurring dreams about Hickey still being alive, usually living incognito at some remote location or living somewhere under an alias. To this day I have those dreams.

As a teenager, I don't believe I had the capacity to realize that the accident wouldn't have happened had we not been drinking. At the time, there were no recovery homes; in fact, the word recovery wasn't being used yet. There was Alcoholics Anonymous, but in those days meetings were occupied primarily with old men who'd been drinking for years. A youngster like me wouldn't have considered going to an AA meeting, much less admitting to a drinking problem. During the sixties, I was arrested around 17 times, all of them convictions except maybe one or two.

I remember cruising Main Street a few months after Hickey's death in my '58 Chevy and listening to the Beatles sing "*I Want to Hold Your Hand*." My grief was subsiding and times were getting better. I was still a relatively clean-cut kid with a nice car and lots of dates, but I was on the road to becoming the *scumbag* that the criminal justice system thought I was. As I mentioned earlier, whites and reds were plentiful. One of my friends, Sherman bought jars of a thousand to sell. He also picked up quite a habit, taking about a hundred pills a day. He used whites to get up and reds to get down. I remember comparing the euphoria of the red/white combination to an orgasm. It wasn't long, however, before Sherman started his downhill spiral with heroin.

Steve and I left Sherman's house one night where we'd been dropping reds and whites and smoking pot. We pulled off the highway between Barstow and Lenwood onto a dirt road and started rolling joints and listening to the radio. To make a long story short, we were arrested for marijuana possession—my first drug charge.

Narcotics Anonymous was around by this time, but not in Barstow. Would I have gone to meetings if there were? No. In my mind, I didn't have a problem with using drugs and alcohol—other people had a problem with me using drugs and alcohol. I retained that attitude for another 25 years.

Officer Montoya, the cop who arrested me for curfew on my Cushman Eagle, was my instructor for the Law Enforcement course at Barstow College. The following semester, at the time of my arrest, I was enrolled in 'Law Enforcement II.' Officer Monds—a local highway patrolman, was the instructor. The next class session after my arrest, Monds called me up to his desk and said, "John, in light of your recent arrest, I strongly suggest that you drop this course." He wasn't suggesting, he was telling, so I dropped the course, and that was the end of my college career at Barstow College in the early 60s.

Monds didn't have the right to ask me to drop the class, but it didn't occur to me to ignore or challenge him. Demoralized as I was, I meekly complied. Officers Montoya and Monds, however, would also get *their* day in court about a year or two later. They were both fired from their jobs as police officers because they were caught expropriating government funds, and the charges had something to do with teaching Law Enforcement courses at Barstow College. Although I'd never heard the phrase *poetic justice*, that's how I looked at it.

That wasn't the only time there was poetic justice in Barstow concerning law enforcement officers who arrested me. In 1962, I was riding with my dad on patrol and tagging doors for him, when a call came over the police radio that there was a burglary in progress at Hartwick's Market. We were close, so we parked across the street to watch the action. The Barstow Police arrived, got out of their squad cars with guns, and surrounded the building. A couple officers were also on the roof. The police radio in my dad's patrol car was transmitting continually. About a half-hour later the officers captured and arrested four men. The Augean stable of our local police department was front-page news in the newspaper the following morning:

BARSTOW POLICE ARREST FOUR OF THEIR OWN ON BURGLARY CHARGES

Art Grin, the officer who arrested me for DUI on my Cushman, was one of the burglars. While I waited a year pending court on my weed possession case, my friend Jon and I started spending a couple evenings a week at a friend's apartment. Glen's wife was pregnant, so she didn't partake, but Jon, Glen, and I loved the downer euphoria that sap gave us.

Sap was our nickname for Robitussun AC cough syrup. The AC stood for added codeine. Until October 1966 in California, under the Controlled Substances Act, any adult could go into a pharmacy and purchase whatever exempt narcotic preparation they wanted. All that was required was a signature in an exempt narcotic registry. This requirement was to keep people like us from purchasing more than one exempt within a 24 hour period. LSD, by the way, was made illegal on the same bill that ended the availability of exempt narcotics. Prior to that, anybody could manufacture, possess, or sell acid.

The Controlled Substances Act was passed when drugs were first classified. Schedule 1 substances are those having a high potential for abuse, and having no medical use, such as heroin, marijuana (then), and cocaine. Schedule II substances, such as Morphine, Dilaudid, Demerol, Oxycontin, and Percodan, also have a high potential for abuse, but they have medical uses. Schedule III substances such as Tylenol with codeine, Doriden, and various hydrocodone preparations for bronchitis like Tussionex, Citra Forte, and Hycodan have an abuse potential less than those in schedules I and II. Schedule IV substances such as Chloral Hydrate, Placidyl (greenie meanies), and most tranquilizers such as Valium and Xanax have a potential for abuse less than those in schedule III. I'll refer again to drug scheduling in a later chapter. Schedule V substances have a potential for abuse less than those in schedule IV, and consist of those preparations formerly known as exempt narcotics.

Barstow's population today is only about 23,000. Its population in the sixties was about 15,000; therefore, it didn't have many pharmacies, so we weren't able to hit the sap stores very often. At that time in California, sap came in four ounce bottles.

One night Jon and I brought an over-the-counter preparation called Asthmadore to share with Glen. It was supposed to be burnt or smoked to relieve asthma symptoms. The recreational affects of Asthmadore were so "out there" that they were often unbelievable. We'd never tried it but we'd heard about it. Goat told me that he found himself sitting in chairs that weren't there and talking to people who weren't there and other crazy situations. Soon we'd find out for ourselves. Each of us took a heaping tablespoon of the gray powder. We'd also drank some sap, and after a couple hours of listening to records, and smoking cigarettes and pot, Glen's wife went to bed

Glen arose from his chair, kissed her goodnight, and then returned to his chair to resume his nod. A couple minutes after the bedroom door closed, Jon arose from his chair and walked into Glen's bedroom. Glen and I just looked at each other, dumbfounded. When Glen opened the bedroom door, Jon was just standing there with a blank look on his face. Glen said, "What the fuck are you doing, Jon?"

Jon kind of snapped out of it momentarily and said, "Oh, I thought I was in an elevator." Then he walked back to his chair and continued his nod. We thought he was just trying to be funny, and it was to me, but it damn sure wasn't to Glen. A couple minutes later, Jon, again coming way out of left field, made a statement that made no sense. We laughed, but with reservations. For one thing, sap didn't put people in a jovial mood where laughter is the order of the day. It's just the opposite.

When we were on sap and people spoke to us, we'd answer as briefly as possible so we could return to our high. Often the curt replies offended people. Jon kept it up, however, and soon his antics weren't funny anymore. We didn't know what the hell was going on with him. We thought it couldn't be the Asthmadore because we weren't carrying on like Jon was. After awhile, Glen didn't insinuate; he bluntly asked us to leave.

After we were in Jon's '55 Pontiac getting ready to leave, he just sat behind the wheel not saying anything. Finally I said, "Let's go."

"We have to wait for Glen," he said in all sincerity.

"Glen went to bed, man. Let's go."

"We have to wait for Glen, I said."

I became more irritated, I said, "dammit, let's go. Glen asked us to leave. He's not coming with us."

In a whisper like he was telling me a secret, he leaned over and said, "He told me he wants to get away from his wife."

I started getting more irritated and said, "What the fuck's wrong with you?"

Calmly and somewhat offended, he straightened up, looked over at me with a wrinkled forehead and replied, "Nothing, what's wrong with you?"

We were still sitting in the driveway when I noticed someone peeking out of Glen's window. Finally, I yelled at him, "Start the fuckin car and let's go!"

He looked at me as though having another moment of clarity, started the car and backed out of Glen's driveway. Then he stopped, put it in park, stepped on the emergency brake, and turned off the motor. I was beside myself. "Jon, we're sitting crossways in the middle of the street, let's go."

"I told you, we have to wait for Glen."

After a couple more minutes of waiting in the middle of the street I asked him to let me drive. Finally, when he saw that he might lose his position of control behind the wheel, he started the car and drove into the Ben Hur gas station down the street where he worked. Glen was the manager of the station. The graveyard attendant, whom he didn't know, came out and asked, "Can I help you?"

"Are the broads here yet?" Jon asked.

"What broads?"

I shook Jon's arm and said, "C'mon Jon, he doesn't know what the hell you're talking about and neither do I."

He shrugged me off and said to the attendant, "You know, they're supposed to be here—the broads. Are they here yet?"

After what seemed like an eternity I finally persuaded him to go. We left the attendant standing there looking perplexed. Leaving the station, Jon drove off the curb and started driving on the wrong side of Main Street. We were approaching a red light, so I told him to run it, turn left and go up Barstow Road. I figured it was better to run the red light, than to sit on the wrong side of Main Street.

On our way up Barstow Road I was temporarily relieved because it was a straight shot from there to the top of the hill where we'd be turning. My reprieve, however, was short-lived. John just stopped driving and started playing with a string hanging from the headliner. I grabbed the wheel and told him to pull over. Then he had another moment of clarity and was okay for a block or two, then he quit driving again, and started fiddling with something on the seat cover. He quit driving a couple more times before we stopped at the signal. After making the right turn on Virginia Way, I tried to talk him into spending the night at my house.

"No," he said, "I have business to take care of."

When we arrived at the stop sign, I was two houses away from home, so I exited the car, shook my head and said, "Okay fine, happy trails," and watched him drive away.

The next morning I went to Glen's station for gas. As Glen approached my window he asked, "Did you hear about Jon?"

"I'm afraid to ask," I replied.

"He's in the nut house."

"I can't imagine why," I said shaking my head.

Glen and I weren't affected by the Asthmador for some reason, but Jon went over the deep end. When he was released, he remembered everything that happened, which is common after going south on this stuff. Recounting to me everything that he and I went through, John said that his experience at the time was real to him. He really thought Glen was supposed to ditch his wife and join us. Then he told me what happened after he dropped me off: he ran into the side of a house two doors down from me. When the resident came out to investigate, he found Jon standing there with joints in his hand. Jon asked the man, "What should I do with these?"

The man said, "I don't know. Throw them away I guess."

Jon threw them on the street where he stood.

When the investigating police officer asked Jon what happened, Jon started counting change back to him. The officer cuffed him and took him to the hospital rather than jail. He was told to sit down, and then the officer left for a couple minutes. When he returned Jon was gone. He'd wandered into a patient's room and after pumping the bed up, he tried to charge the patient a dollar for changing a tire.

After hearing this story, most people have trouble believing it, or they think it's grossly exaggerated. I assure all of the doubters that it is true. This wasn't my only experience with someone taking Asthmadore. One day Jon gave a friend of ours, Bruce, *two* heaping tablespoons. Bruce started feeling the effects in my bedroom at my parents' house. When he started looking for his girlfriend in an encyclopedia, under the bed, and between the pillow and the pillow case, I told Jon that I wasn't going through another Asthmadore trip again. "You take Bruce and get the fuck outta here. I've had my fill of Asthmadore!" And away they went.

I never wanted anything more to do with Asthmadore. It has since been taken off the market, and I don't think belladonna (the active ingredient) is used any longer in pharmaceutical preparations. Both Jon and Bruce were hedonistic, recalcitrant young men who were easily influenced, but after their relative experiences with Asthmadore, they both remained inveterate criminalized drug addicts. Bruce ended up dead and Jon will surface again in a later chapter.

Why did I tell this story? Because phrases such as 'drug addicts will go to any lengths to get high' doesn't really get the point across. The things addicts go through are not deterrents. No matter what, until they've had enough, nothing or nobody can convince them to stop.

CHAPTER SIX

Puer Aeternus

Puer aeternus is a Latin term translated as eternal boy and used in mythology to refer to a child-god who is forever young. Psychologically, the term refers to an older man whose emotional life has remained at an adolescent level—a puerile nature. Using emotional logic, addicts, like adolescents usually live for the moment. Emotionally, addicts act like adolescents and are often described as adolescent in behavior and attitude. After all, many issues addicts struggle with are the same issues that face adolescents, with the difference being that addicts stay trapped in an adolescent stage as long as their addiction is in progress. At 20 years old, my adolescence should've been transforming into the more responsible lifestyle of adulthood, but instead I remained trapped in adolescent psychology, otherwise referred to in depth psychology as personifying the *puer aeternus* archetype.

Carl Jung's theory of the collective unconscious is a repository of archetypes. An archetype is an unconscious behavioral pattern. The archetypes of the collective unconscious can be thought of as a universal gene pool of behavioral patterns that have always been and will always be a part of the human condition. One example of an archetype is the good mother—we're all familiar with the women who epitomize motherhood. There's also the bad mother archetype—we all know her. Jungian psychology focuses on other archetypes such as the anima and animus. With the anima being the feminine side of man, and the animus being the masculine side of woman, Jung also wrote extensively on the shadow archetype, which is the dark side of humanity. Whether we want to acknowledge it or not, we all have a dark side.

The archetypes are bi-polar. The negative *puer* is characterized by a poor adjustment to daily demands, a failure to set stable goals and to make lasting achievements in accord with these goals, and a proclivity for intense but short-lived romantic attachments. The positive *puer* is characterized by noble idealism, a fertile imagination, spiritual insight, and frequently by remarkable talent. Unfortunately, as this book makes obvious, I personified the negative *puer*, as do most addicts.

Jon and I wanted to get out of Barstow, so we took our puerile natures and moved in with a bunch of guys, eleven of them, in Paramount, California. Big Head was working at a tool and die factory, a job he kept for several years before moving his family to Barstow. He got Jon and me jobs there as punch press operators, and we rode to work and back with him because we didn't have a car yet.

Jody, another old friend, sold me a '50 Plymouth for fifty bucks. I then enrolled full time at Long Beach City College, but smoking pot every night with Jon wasn't conducive to student life, so I dropped out before the first semester was over. After two failed attempts at college, I put the idea of college behind me because I didn't consider myself college material.

All 13 of us were never in the apartment at the same time, but it was still congested periodically. We were all forced to move after Big Head accidentally set fire to the apartment by passing out with a lit cigarette in his hand. I was blissfully asleep when I was suddenly awakened by firefighters storming through the apartment. The apartment was ruined, so we all went our separate ways. Jon, Big Head, and I rented a house nearby.

We partied hard in that house for several months and made a veritable mess of it. None of us wanted to wash dishes or clean up. Our poor adjustment to daily demands seemed to come naturally. With "*Heart of Stone*" by the Rolling Stones playing on the radio, I remember looking around our house one day thinking, *look at this fucking pigsty. The stench from that sink is gross, there's dirty clothes laying all over the place, and the floors look like people have been shitting on em.* When my moment of clarity was over, I went back to what I was doing and didn't lift a finger to clean it up. My dad showed up for a visit, really to see how I was living, and left the next day completely disgusted. If the word *scumbag* was in his vocabulary, he probably used it to describe his son and his friends.

Big Head didn't do drugs anymore but he was a practicing alcoholic. One day he came back to my bedroom and caught Jody, Jon, and me smoking pot. "What the fuck are you guys doing?"

"What's it look like?" said Jody while holding his breath and offering him a hit.

"You guys get out of here with that shit," grumbled Big Head, "I don't want to go to jail because you guys are stupid."

"Here," I said after taking a hit, "have some. It's really good shit."

"I'm trying to stay away from that shit, and I don't appreciate you fuckers bringing it in here, now get the fuck out of here!"

Big Head paid most of the rent, so he was justified in assuming the position of head of household. Jon and I both were fired from our jobs, which gave Big Head further impetus to ask us to move out.

We moved into a duplex next door to Glen and his wife, who was conveniently living in nearby North Long Beach. Having been sapheads in Barstow together, Jon, Glen, and I started hitting the sap pretty heavy. There was no running out of pharmacies in L.A. We stayed as high as our money allowed. We even found an unethical pharmacist who didn't care what we were using it for. At this pharmacy, I'd walk in and ask for a bottle of Robitussun AC. I'd sign the register, pay for it and leave. When Jon went in after me, the pharmacist already had another bottle sitting out with the book ready to sign, and the process would be repeated with Glen. We signed a different name every day to keep the register looking like different people were buying it.

When Jon and I found a couple of teenage girlfriends, whom I'll call Carol and Debbie, we lightened up on the sap for awhile. They were attracted to older guys with their own apartment—they could get laid in a bed instead of the back seat of a car. Our sex lives were great, but our financial state wasn't. We told Carol and Debbie that we'd have to move unless we could find a way to pay our rent. The girls didn't want us to leave, so they stole money from their parents and paid the rent two months in a row. Not long after the second month, however, we started hitting the sap hard again. Usually we'd get high next door at Glen's place, but once in a while when he wasn't home, we'd have to get high at our apartment. When we were stoned on sap, we didn't want anything to do with the girls. "Look, Debbie," I explained, "we're not angry with you. We're just loaded on sap, which makes us appear like we're angry."

"That's right," confirmed Jon. "It's probably better if you weren't around us when we're loaded."

"You guys are using that as an excuse. We paid your fucking rent, now you don't want anything to do with us," argued Carol.

That wasn't true: However, we wanted away from them even more when they screwed up our high by nagging. Because of their nagging, we'd rather be loaded than deal with them to have sex. Our rent was paid for another month so we ended up dumping them by not answering the door or hiding at Glen's apartment. When our rent was due again, we returned to Barstow. It was time to start my 120 days for the weed possession.

At Glen Helen, I was not placed in minimum security like I was when I was there with Goat and Dirty Dick in '63. Drug offenders and other security risks were remanded to maximum security where 50 of us lived in one big cell—a big dorm with bars. Again I was with friends from Barstow and I also met new ones. Having typing skills, I landed a clerical job that came with fringe benefits, like appointing special bunks to friends, manipulating TV schedules, and getting people appointed to various jobs. Again, I really didn't mind being there. It wasn't like punishment, except for being away from the streets where I could do anything I wanted. I even contacted the judge who sentenced me to see if I could stay longer instead of serving probation. He denied my request.

Jail wasn't much of a threat since the first time I landed there and had so much fun with Huck. After two stretches at Glen Helen, doing county time was neither a threat, nor a deterrent to drug use and associated crimes.

I returned to Barstow when I was released. It was 1965, the year the Rolling Stones were fined for urinating on a wall, the year Malcolm X was shot to death, and the year I took my first shot of heroin. As soon as I pulled the needle out of my arm, I went to the nearest toilet bowl and dumped my guts out. By that time, many of my friends were using heroin periodically, and some of them were starting to develop habits. I'd try and try to use it like they did, but it didn't agree with me. For some reason, I had a sensitive resistance to it, so I never became *physically* addicted to it. I did, however, use it periodically over the next 20 years. I wanted to like it, and I did enjoy the high, but it just made me too nauseous to use it on a continual basis.

Before disposable syringes came out, diabetics kept a permanent syringe and a store of needles that were available at pharmacies. Junkies, however, made their own syringes called binkies. In the Murine Eye Drops package, along with the bottle of eye drops was a separate eyedropper. We'd put the needle on the end of the eyedropper. After putting the heroin in a spoon and adding water, we used a lighter or matches to cook it until the powder dissolved and the mixture started to boil, filling the room with a sticky sweet odor. Next we dropped a piece of cotton into the liquid, and after squeezing the rubber plunger of the eyedropper, we put the needle into the cotton, then let go of the plunger. The eyedropper would then fill up leaving the cotton dry. We held the end of the needle so nothing could leak out, and then shook the liquid to the fore of the eyedropper. We tied off our arms with a belt or whatever was available, inject the needle into a vein, wait for blood to register in the eye dropper, and then squeeze the plunger. Bingo, instant rush. For me, however, it was Bingo, instant rush, and then nausea or vomiting. Sometimes it was worse than others but the nausea, at some degree, was always there.

When I reported to my new PO, I remember distinctly what Mr. Hayward said to me: "John, you better walk a straight line, because if you don't, you're going to fall. And if you fall, you're going to fall hard."

Immediately my walls went up and with a cocky attitude I said, "What are you going to do, watch my every step and hope you can catch me doing something so you can put me back in jail?"

"Here are your terms of probation. I suggest you read them and pay heed."

The first rule said, violate no law. "Mr. Hayward, this first term can be grounds for putting me in jail for walking against a red light."

"Then don't walk against a red light," he said with firm conviction.

"Why don't you just lock me up now, because there's no way I can terminate this probation with you breathing down my neck?"

"John, I don't like your attitude."

"I don't like yours either... *Sir*!"

I don't believe my attitude was unique among rebellious youngsters. Of course, what was behind the rebelliousness was chemical dependency. Take rebellion out of the equation, and there'd probably be a normally functioning youth either working on a college degree or working his way up a corporate ladder. There are those who get into trouble without the help of drugs and alcohol, but how many prisons would they have to close in this country if all of the people in them were released who were there, directly or indirectly, as a result of the use of drugs and/or alcohol?

~

A couple years later I hooked up with an old friend and we decided to go live in Reno. We loaded everything into Herby's '61 Mercury and headed for Vegas. Knowing that we wouldn't be able to score drugs in Reno, at least for a while, we wanted to take a stash with us. We already had some pot, but we wanted more, so we started hitting the drug stores for a supply of sap; however, for some reason, pharmacists in Nevada wouldn't sell the Robitussin AC brand, so we settled for the nasty tasting Turpin Hydrate brand. Furthermore, Nevada only sold it in two ounce bottles. Reno was a much smaller city, so we knew we'd be even more limited there.

Searching for sap took place on the same day that Herby and Martha remarried. Martha had divorced him because of his heroin habit, but since they had a daughter, they remarried so Herby could avoid the draft. I was conveniently the best man. After we took Martha back home in Vegas, and picked up a few more bottles of sap, we pulled over to drink a bottle. "Okay Herby, here goes... chug, chug, gulp. Ohhhh, shit! Yuck, whew, oh man—that shit makes my eyes water. Damn, that's some foul tasting shit!"

"You fucking wimp, watch how a real man takes it... chug, chug, gulp. Ohhhhh fuck! God damn, whew—[shakes his head] Damn that shit's nasty!"

I smiled, laughed, and said, "Wow, that was really manly."

Herby later developed a system to counteract the awful taste of turp. First, we opened a soda. Then took a stick of gum and chewed it until it was juicy, and then set it down. We took a drink of soda, quickly set it down and drank the entire bottle of turp as fast as possible; then we'd take another big drink of soda as a chaser, and then put the partly chewed gum in our mouths and chewed it vigorously. We hoped that going through all that was enough to keep us from gagging, or worse yet, throwing up. The only reason I went into such detail with this process is to demonstrate again the lengths addicts will go to get high. When people are in recovery, staying clean has to be the number one priority in their lives. For practicing addicts and/or alcoholics, getting high is the number one priority in their lives.

In Reno, as usual, I went from job to job. Herby even landed me a job where he worked, but I ended up quitting because I didn't want to do something that my supervisor asked.

Reno's climate took some getting used to, especially for us, because we'd been in the desert all of our lives. Reno was green and beautiful in the summer, and there was a river running through town as well as a couple small lakes. However, in the winter, we scraped ice off our windshield in the mornings, and if that weren't bad enough, we needed to drive with kid gloves because of the icy roads. People not used to those conditions can easily get into car accidents. For one who was known for liking the sound of metal against metal, it's amazing that I never once had a collision during the eight or nine months that I lived there.

Herby didn't make a lot of money, and my contribution wasn't enough for us to live very well. We rented a small studio apartment, and the L shaped sofa made into two single beds. Once we ran out of sap and pot, we drank a lot of shake-shake. When we went grocery shopping, we bought the bare necessities for survival along with ten bottles of White Port and ten cans of lemon juice each.

One night after each of us drank a bottle of shake-shake (Whit Port and lemon juice), we went to the Washoe County Fair. Just for shits and giggles, we sneaked up behind people and hissed loudly into their ears—startling them—and then we walked away laughing. After Herby hissed into a woman's ear, her boyfriend or husband attacked him and knocked him down. While they were fighting, the police attacked Herby with Billy clubs. For whatever reason, they didn't bother the other guy. Perhaps Herby's drunkenness was obvious, or perhaps they saw Herby hiss into the woman's ear. Herby gave me his keys from the back end of a paddy wagon, and I drove home. How many times I've driven in that condition is astronomical, and the number of cars I've wrecked driving drunk is astounding, but I made it home that night. After I was up and around the next morning, I hired a bondsman and bailed Herby out of jail.

CHAPTER SEVEN

Squeaky

While Herby was working I used his car to look for work. One day while I was out looking, I was written a citation for speeding in a school zone. Herby went with me to pay the fine. On the sidewalk outside the court house, this strange man approached Herby and started talking to him like they were long lost buddies: "Hewwo Herby, how ya been? Wow, it's willy nice seein ya. I jus been walkin wound here twying to wook busy, heh heh heh."

With a speech impediment making him sound like Elmer Fudd, the stranger carried on like that for a couple minutes before saying, "Say Herby, why don't you bail me outta here? It onwy costs ten bucks and I will pay you back wite away."

I asked, "Do you know where I could get work?"

His reply was, "Oh yeah, you can wook wit me—you can be my bwush man. Ya see, I cwean windows aw ova town. I'm Squeaky da window cweaner. If you wook for me, I do the squeegee and you do da bwush—you'd be my bwush man."

Herby asked "Do know where we could get any pot?"

"Oh yeah, I can get aw you want. I know people aw ova da pwace."

Herby told him to hang on for a few minutes while we paid the fine for my speeding citation. On the way in I looked at Herby and asked, "I thought you didn't know anybody in Reno?"

"I don't. I met him in jail. I got a kick out of talking to him, but he seemed to get on a lot of people's nerves in there."

After I paid my fine, I said, "Hey, it might be fun having a weirdo like that around, plus I could go to work for him."

"I'm not sure I believe he has a business."

"So what? It's only ten bucks?"

"Fuck it, I don't give a shit. If he becomes a problem, we can just get rid of him."

We bailed him out. The jailer yelled back into the cell blocks, "Hey, someone's bailin' Squeak out!" To our surprise, there were a lot of hoorays and whistling and carrying on. Apparently, the officers and inmates alike were glad to be rid of a nuisance. After witnessing all the commotion, Herby and I started wondering what we'd gotten ourselves into. Trustees were not allowed to leave the building and walk around on the streets asking people to bail them out, but the jailers were obviously willing to break the rules to get rid of Squeaky.

The weather in Reno was cool but clear and the sun was shining, a nice day to start a new career in the window cleaning business. After parking Herby's car, Squeaky grabbed his squeegees and rags and put them in his back pockets. He grabbed his bucket, pole, and brush, and we walked up to his customer's shop windows. He demonstrated how I was supposed to use the brush on the first window pane, and then handed me the brush for the next pane. About half way through the pane, he grabbed the brush out of my hand and said, "No, no bwush man, not like dat, like dis." Then he demonstrated again.

Damn, I don't know if I can handle this. I feel like knocking him out. Suddenly a short, tired looking, redheaded shopkeeper came out of the front door and started yelling, "What the fuck you doing? If you think you can stop doing my windows for a god-damn month and then show up when you feel like it, then you're out of your rabbit-ass mind!"

Appearing shocked and bewildered, Squeaky just looked at him at first, and then before the shopkeeper could continue his tirade, Squeaky screamed back: "If you shu-up a minute, maybe I tell you why I ain't been awound." The temperamental shopkeeper lightened up and Squeaky continued: "Joey," said Squeaky, "I was in da hospital, bwodder, I coun't make it."

Squeaky effectively made his point with some convincing facial expressions and body language, because it silenced Joe completely. "Okay Squeak, I'm sorry, I didn't know."

What the shopkeeper also didn't know was what an effective liar and con artist Squeaky was. "I jus had sugery a week ago, Joey, and I willy shoun't be here woking wight now, but I din't wanna wet you down, ya know?"

As if the shopkeeper didn't feel bad enough, Squeaky really started pouring it on. By the time Squeaky stopped carrying on, the shopkeeper believed his lies and was practically eating out of his hand. Once we were in the car, with his crooked smile and bizarre laugh, he said, "Dat's da way ya do bisness, bwush man."

"Squeak?"

"What?" Squeaky replied.

"Did you know that lies go traveling around the world while truth is still putting its boots on?"

"What's dat mean?"

"Never mind."

During the first year of Squeaky's window cleaning career, he fell off of the Mapes Hotel in Reno cleaning windows. Amazingly enough, he survived. As a result, he had four outstanding disabilities: a lame leg, a speech impediment, a crooked smile, and a severe case of insanity, but Squeaky's customers just attributed his eccentric behavior to a characteristic and unorthodox personality that was genuinely entertaining if being around him too long wasn't required.

Squeaky needed his customers' money to maintain his alcohol addiction and gambling habit on pin ball machines, so when he'd take a leave of absence for jail time or whatever, he hoodwinked his customers into believing whatever he told them. He was a very convincing liar and had a jovial and amicable personality when he wanted to.

At the next stop, I started brushing a window. Again, he jerked the brush out of my hand and said, "God damnit bwush man, you don't do it wite. Watz wong wit you? If you don't do da bwush wite, I'm gonna hafta fire you."

"You can't fire me until you pay us back the ten dollars for bailing you out."

"Don't wemind me. Just do da bwush wite."

Fortunately, by the time we arrived at the next shop, I was doing better with the brush. After we finished the job, he wrote out a receipt and went in to collect. After a short conversation and reassuring his customer of his faithful return, we left for his next customer. I was surprised to find that he was living up to his claims of having a business.

We went to two or three more customers where the same process occurred. Then after doing the windows at the next stop, he presented his receipt to the shopkeeper as usual.

“What's this for, sir?” the shopkeeper asked.

“Wha ya mean, I jus did da windows, sir. I been doin em fo years.”

“I bought this business a month ago, and I’ve arranged for our own maintenance.”

A minor setback. Squeaky then started pouring on the charm: “Oh I'm sowwy sir—I din't kno.” And with a big crooked smile, he continued, “Da windows wook vewy nice, don't you think? And sir, Squeaky neva, eva weaves stweeks or smudges, and my pwices are da best in weeno.”

I was impressed when we walked away with a steady account that paid more than what he was getting from the former owners. He knew the business had new owners and saw the opportunity to get more money for the job.

Later that day, we went to a super market and he went in and made the deal. The job took us more than two hours, and he was paid well for it. After we ate lunch and did a few more jobs, he directed me back to the same super market. Sitting in the parking lot, I asked, “What are you doing here again?”

Incredulously he replied, “I'm witeing a weceipt, what's it wook wike?” While getting out of the car, he looked at me like I was a germ and went back in the store. When he came walking out with that big crooked smile on his face, it was obvious what he had done. This time he didn't get a steady customer; in fact, he blew the chance to do the windows ever again, because he collected twice for the same job—once from the day manager who was on duty when we did the windows, and again this time. The evening manager paid him for doing the windows before, so if he wanted to confirm whether Squeaky did the windows or not, all he needed to do was ask one of the checkers that was still on duty.

Squeaky was a con man and he conned Herby and me as well. We let him sleep on the floor of our little studio apartment. When I started asking for some of the money we were making, he would make promises that he never kept. He said that he needed to pay back money he owed or that he needed to make a payment on this or that or he needed it to buy more equipment and supplies, promising faithfully that once his immediate debts were paid, the money would start rolling in. He gave us just enough to keep us from kicking him out. He also disappeared in the evenings for a few hours.

Squeaky directed me to a really nice nightclub in Reno called the Lemon Tree, the kind with a cover charge. He seemed to be acquainted with the manager. When he talked the manager into allowing him to test his new dance floor treatment, the manager agreed. Squeaky treated a small section of the floor, and then asked the manager to test it. After doing so, the manager was impressed and asked how much. Squeaky told him that he could sell him a gallon for $25.00. The manager appeared pleased with the price. Squeaky told him that he'd need to go to his warehouse to get it. Of course Squeaky didn't have a warehouse.

Instead, he went into a grocery store and bought a 25-cent bottle of floor wax. When he was back in the car, he poured it into one of his window-cleaning solution bottles, and then filled the rest with window cleaning solution. We returned to the Lemon Tree and Squeaky was paid $25.00

Herby and I periodically went to the bars and drank with Squeaky. He was well known in Reno, but we couldn't help noticing that many people didn't like talking to him for very long. He was on our nerves too, but we felt he was worth it because neither of us had ever associated with anyone quite as disturbed. There was never a dull moment around him—we just had to put up with some of his irksome idiosyncrasies, character flaws, and drinking and gambling habit. We had drinking habits of our own, so we couldn't really hold that against him. Moreover, we were impressed with the many facets of his con-man repertoire.

By this time Herby and I knew how often, and where we could get sap, so we'd occasionally get some while Squeaky was taking a shower or otherwise occupying himself in the evenings. One evening when we were loaded on sap, Squeaky asked, "Watz wong wit you guys. You jus sit dare wike yer sweeping."

We explained to him, like Jon and I had explained to Carol and Debbie, how sap affected us. Eventually, he'd just leave when we were high. "I'm gettin outta here, you guys awe boring and gwumpy." It was times like these that he'd go off and get drunk and gamble. He didn't like being around us when we were smoking pot either because we laughed at him too much. "You guys willy hurt my feewings when you waugh at me wike dat."

We finally figured Squeaky out when it came to money. One night after ordering dinner in a casino restaurant, he left for a while. By the time the food arrived he still hadn't returned, so I went looking for him. I found him at a pinball machine, and he wasn't about to leave until he won some of the money back he'd just invested. I went back and told Herby what I observed. We ate our dinner, paid for it, and then went into the casino, leaving his food untouched. When we approached Squeaky at the pinball machine, Herby commented, “Hey, I hope you’re not gambling on the fifty dollars I owe the bail bondsman.”

Squeaky said. “No pwobwem, Herby, I got da money.”

It wasn’t long before it became painfully obvious that he gambled away Herby’s money. He lost everything. That was the last straw. We told Squeaky that he was on his own and that he could come by the apartment whenever he liked to pick up the rest of his belongings. Herby and I have spent many hours telling people about our escapades with Squeaky da window cweaner. Squeaky will surface again later, *reincarnated*.

We’ve often wondered how different our lives might’ve been when we lived in Reno if we’d have had the money to go over to the Haight-Ashbury district in San Francisco. At that time, neither of us had tried LSD, but we wanted to. It didn’t do any good to ask Squeaky to get it for us because he’d just make promises he wouldn’t keep. However, we found more conventional ways to have fun.

In January of 1967 I asked Herby, “Hey, you wanna celebrate my 22nd birthday with me in a whorehouse?”

He said “No, but I don’t mind if you take my car.” Prostitution was legal in the neighboring county, and I enjoyed the ride over there. It was certainly fun while I was there; plus I was in good spirits on my way home. I remember listening to Frank Sinatra sing “*That’s Life*.” I thought about how unusual it was for someone like Sinatra to have a top ten hit on the charts when rock groups like the Beatles and Stones were dominating the airways.

Another particular night of fun was when Herby and I were in a bar shooting pool. My quarter was up and the game was for a dollar. I won. Not only did I win, but I was in a cocky mood and every time I made a shot (which was more often than not, a sloppy shot), I’d say something like, “Oh my God, I’m good. I’m so good!” By the time the next game was over, of which I again won, the other players in the room were starting to become annoyed by my arrogance, prompting the next guy to say, “Let’s make it five dollars, hot shot.”

I said, “You got it, sunshine,” and I won again. The fact is, I wasn’t that good of a pool player. I was average and not *nearly* as good as I was that night. It seemed like I was unable to miss. One of the disgruntled players used the phone to call a more experienced player to come down and get me off the table. It didn't do any good because I beat him too. Not only was my cocky attitude annoying them, but Herby was sitting there giggling every time I made a shot, sometimes making remarks such as, "Wow, What a shot! These guys should start praying to you."

Twice more they called people to come down to put an end to my winning, but to no avail—I continually won every game. Some of the shots I made were so obviously sloppy. Anybody with any pool playing experience could see that, but I played it off like it was skill, and Herby laughed and continued with smart-ass remarks. I don't remember how much money I'd won by then, but it was quite a bit. Through eye contact, Herby and I agreed that we should leave. Herby left, and after the next game, I excused myself to go to the rest room, making some snippy remark as I left. As soon as I was back in the car, we sped away from there as fast as we could, laughing all the way home. I'd never played that way before and I never played that way again. We also considered ourselves lucky to have gotten away from there without getting our butts kicked.

Once we were rid of Squeaky, our financial status improved and we moved into a house in nearby Sparks. Because we spent so much time in the bars shooting pool, Herby bought a full size pool table on credit from Sears. There was very little furniture in the house, and none in the living room except the new pool table. Both of us being introverts, we still hadn't made any friends. We spent our evenings getting drunk, smoking pot, shooting pool, and once in a while nodding out on a bottle or two of sap.

A couple weeks after moving into our new house, Herby's wife and daughter came for a visit. The next morning after Herby and his wife spent the night together, they informed me that they were getting back together. He wasn't tied to heroin anymore, so their domestic life could continue as it was before he became strung out. With their family reuniting, it was time for me to leave, so I went back home to my parents in Barstow. The timing was good for my dad, because he needed help with his gold mine venture in the Avawatz Mountains.

CHAPTER EIGHT

The Shadow of Death

My dad's automotive mechanic, Bob, told my dad about a gold mine that his wife's father had worked years before. Bob's father-in-law carried a hundred dollars worth of high grade ore on his back, but the mine was so far up into the mountains that it wasn't worth the physical effort to continue at his advanced age.

Bob and my dad agreed that they could sell their businesses and retire if they could get the ore out of there efficiently. The agreement they made was that of an investor on my dad's part, the mine and the expertise of extracting the ore on Bob's part. By the time I returned from Reno, my dad was getting ready to take up there an old trailer that I'd lived in for awhile in the Los Angeles area.

To get there it was about 40 miles west on highway 127 toward Ash Meadows from Baker, and then left onto a dirt road for about 20 miles. The Avawatz Mountains, where the mine was located, was visible to the left. Then it was left again up a rocky wash for about four miles. After leaving the wash with another left, it was only a couple miles before the walking began. That's where the trailer was going to be parked. The uppermost part of the wash was located on the northeast corner of the Ft. Irwin Army Reservation. The mine was located on the far southeast corner of the Death Valley Monument. Later, there would be an issue regarding trespassing on government property to get to the mine.

My dad was born in 1900, so in 1967 he was 67 years old. In addition, he had a heart blockage, and emphysema and was overweight, so he was incapable of any of the physical labor required. That's why he needed me. "Hey, bub," he said, "I need you to go to the mine with Bob so he can show you how to extract the ore out of the mountain. If something happens to him, you'll need to know how to do it."

I reluctantly agreed. When the time came, old Bob and I and his 10-year-old son drove to Baker, gassed up, and drove to where we couldn't drive any farther. Then we started walking. I wasn't in very good physical condition because I'd been a virtual trash can for chemicals for so long. By the time we made it to the top of the mountain, I was exhausted. However, I wasn't going to let on in front of an old man and a young boy that I was so out of shape that I felt like I was on the verge of collapse.

I expected a conventional gold mine that goes into the side of a mountain, but when we arrived, there was nothing there but a small hole in the ground. Old Bob showed me how to extract the high-grade ore out of the hole. We brought bags and each of us filled one up before we started back down the mountain. Going down wasn't any easier than going up because we were toting ten pounds of ore each. When we finally returned to the truck, we returned to Barstow, and I thought my job was done. I started partying with my friends again until my dad approached me again.

"Hey, bub, I need you to go back to the mine with Bob. We've moved your old trailer up there, and this time you'll be taking mules to haul the ore back down with. You'll be staying a couple days this time."

I said, "Okay Dad, but on one condition. I'm going to need some help this time. That's treacherous and exhausting work getting up there and back. I want you to call Dr. Graybill and tell him that your brother is in town and needs to drive to Oklahoma by Friday. Ask him to write a prescription for thirty tabs of Dexamil."

"You want me to get drugs for you?" he asked.

"Yeah, I do."

"I can't do that."

"Then I can't go up there."

Off I went with 30 tabs of Dexamil, an old man, two pack mules, and some mining equipment. Again, it was rough driving up that rocky wash, and even rougher up that poor excuse of a road. We stayed in the trailer that night and was up at dawn. The old man made us a couple pieces of French toast each, and I dropped a couple dexies. We loaded the mules with empty ore bags, food, and digging equipment, and then started our hike to the top.

When we finally arrived and rested awhile, old Bob pointed down the face of the mountain to where we could see the first dirt road that we came in on. "Johnny, " he said, "in order to make this venture profitable and not be encroaching on government property, we're hoping to make a road up here, without having to drive all the way around and over all that rough terrain. That and bringing pack mules up here to haul the ore out will put a heavy strain on our profit margin. So, I want you to walk down the face of this mountain and try to visualize a road being made straight up here from that road down there that we came in on. Skip and my boy will be coming up this afternoon with more supplies, so after you reach the road, they'll pick you up. Do you think you can do that?"

"Yeah," I replied feeling pleasantly wired, "just walk down this mountain and visualize a road up here. How hard is that?"

"That's right, and Skip will pick you up on the road and bring you back."

Damn good thing I'm wired, I thought. I filled my canteen and started down the face of the mountain—no big deal, right? It took me about two hours, and it looked to me like a road *could* be made up there, though it wouldn't be easy. When I made it to the road, I started walking toward the wash. Four hours later I made it to the wash but still no Skip. *Well, he has to come this way too, so I'll just walk up the wash. Damn, I hope he gets here soon.*

Up to this time I was drinking water as my thirst demanded, but after trudging up that wash for a while, it occurred to me that any number of conditions could keep Skip from making it. He was already late, so I started to conserve my water, only taking small sips when I needed it. I was also starting to get tired. Whenever I could find shade, which wasn't very often, I rested for 15 or 20 minutes. Before I knew it, dark was approaching and still no Skip. *Damn, I'm really getting tired. Fuck! I left my stash of Dexies in the trailer. Oh no, I hadn't figured on Skip not showing up. I better find a safe spot to sleep. I don't want to step on a rattlesnake or scorpion walking up this fucking wash at night.*

I cleared a spot and surrounded myself with rocks for some reason, and then used a bigger rock for a pillow. *Damn, it's starting to get cold and all I have on is this flimsy t-shirt. I need to find a better spot—a place more protective from the elements and critters.* I found a spot on the side of the wash where two big rocks came together like a V. After pulling my arms inside of my t-shirt and squeezing between those rocks, I curled up into the fetal position. I managed to sleep sporadically until around five o'clock in the morning when it really started getting cold. *Damn, I'm shivering so bad there's no way I can sleep any longer. Shit, I better start walking or even running—maybe I could even break a sweat.* So I jogged as far as I could and then walked for an hour or so. *Fuck, my endurance isn't what it was yesterday morning when I was jacked up on Dexies. I'm having to stop more often and now the heat is coming on again and my water isn't going to last much longer.*

After another hour, I started wondering: *Have I gone up the wrong wash? Is Skip already up there? Am I going to fucking die here?* With these thoughts, among more ominous ones, I started to panic. *I wouldn't be the first fucking gold miner to die in these mountains. Hey, maybe there are people within hearing distance in another wash or on some road nearby*, so I started yelling as loud as I could, "Heeeeelp! Heeeelp!" After doing that for about ten minutes, I started walking again. *It's hotter than hell, and a lot hotter today than yesterday*. Then I took off my T-shirt and stuck in into my back pocket, taking it out periodically to wipe the sweat off my face. After another mile or so, I sat on a rock in the middle of the wash. There wasn't any shade for as far as I could see in either direction.

I had precious little water left. When I started walking again, I needed to stop more often because the cracks in my dry throat were screaming for water, but I could only dampen them. Actually, there wasn't enough to take a *drink*. Again my mortality became glaringly threatened. *This is no fucking way to die*! Desperately hoping to be rescued, I started looking for low flying aircraft. *Goddamn, surely the old man has a search party out for me.* I was scared for my life in a way I'd never been scared before. *My dad has sent me to hell for all the shit I've put him and my mom through. If I get out of this, I'll quit drugs and alcohol. I ain't fucking praying though—just because I might die is no reason to start believing in fairy tales.*

After walking, very slowly I might add, my back started feeling burnt from the sun, so I reached back to grab my t-shirt. *Oh No, It's gone!* I turned around and looked back down the wash. *Fuck that, I'm not going back down there, no way, not away from my destination. It doesn't matter anyway.* I *can never walk that far without water—I'm almost out. Damn! I'm really gonna die. I'm going to die without having any kids. Kids? I don't want kids. I don't want a wife either. On second thought, maybe I should get one and settle down. What am I talking about? I'm going to fucking die here. I'm never gonna get to go to the Mardi Gras or visit other countries. I'll be dead. My mom will divorce my dad for killing me. Oh, my poor parents. I'm their only kid.*

By this time the cracks in my throat, caused from being so dry, were coming about every hundred yards. *I'm a fucking mess. Why did I ever agree to this?* I started thinking more about death and what it might be like. *Is there some other kind of life after we die? Is the Christian myth really true? Does our whole life really flash before us? Have we lived other lives?* Very slowly I started walking again, trudging . . . trudging like a caterpillar. When I looked ahead of me, I didn't think I recognized the terrain any longer. *Oh shit, I don't remember that, or that, or . . . Oh fucking No! I passed the old car body where I was supposed to turn. How in the fuck did I miss that?* At that point, my throat was so dry and cracked that I wasn't sure I could walk any farther, but then I thought I noticed something up on the left side of the wash. Although I knew I was walking away from my destination, something was pulling me up the wash a little farther to get a better look. I just hoped my throat wouldn't swell up so badly that I wouldn't be able to breathe at all.

The closer I got, the more I thought I was hallucinating. *Are those really caves on the left side of the wash up there?* The cracks in my throat were so thick, I couldn't walk over ten yards without moistening them with the precious few drops left in my canteen. Continually wiping the sweat off my sunburned face with my hand, I trudged on. *Wow! They are caves—natural fucking caves at that, and finally some shade.*

I also noticed man-made indentations on the other side of the wash. *This part of the wash was once a mining camp I bet*. I approached the first cave, and when I looked inside, I knew that I'd died and went to heaven. There in front of me in all their radiant beauty were five stunningly gorgeous naked women, smiling, and waving for me to come in! No, I'm kidding, but there was water. There were a lot of bugs in the water, but I just swished them away and started filling my canteen. When it was about half full, I tipped it up and poured that cool water down my throat and then poured it all over me. I stayed in that cave for an hour or more resting and recuperating from a virtual near-death experience that I'd never, ever forget. Nor would I forget that place.

After gorging myself with water, I started back down the wash to look for the old car body, but before getting to it, I saw a vehicle in the distance. The closer it came, the clearer I could see my rescuers. When the Jeep reached me, Skip and the old man and his son were in it.

The old man looked as ragged as I felt, so he told me what he'd been through. "Johnny, when Skip didn't show up like he was supposed to, I decided to follow your tracks in hopes of catching you on the road waiting for Skip. I managed to retrace your steps most of the way, and made safe assumptions at other times when your trail wasn't visible. Once I was on the road where Skip was supposed to pick you up, your tracks were a lot easier to follow. Johnny, I walked almost the entire distance that you did. Skip just now picked me up down here on the wash."

I sat there listening. I wasn't in full control of my faculties. Later, Skip and the old man told my dad that I was delirious when they found me. Although I hadn't eaten since the two pieces of French toast before I started walking, I was unable to stomach any food. Part of the reason was probably connected with the Dexies. They were being prescribed at the time for appetite suppression.

The old man continued, "Now Johnny, the most frightening part of *my* walk was when I found mountain lion tracks in your tracks. An animal that could sense your weakened condition was stalking you. After that I started praying that I wouldn't come upon your remains."

Not being capable of fully realizing what he was telling me, I simply replied, "Well, the way I feel, I think that mountain lion did get me." When I finally made it back home, I told my dad what he could do with his gold mine.

On the way back to the trailer, I told them about the springs of water in the caves. Old Bob pulled out a map and pointed to a spot and said, "That's where you were." There was a name for my oasis in the desert: *Cave Spring*. My assumption was correct about it once being a mining camp.

The *Mojave River Valley Museum* is where orientation classes are held for Barstow College field trip courses in archeology. My excitement was understandable, when taking a field trip course 25 years later, I saw an old sign in the museum that read: CAVE SPRING, 4 Miles. I also found a book in the museum entitled, *320 Watering Places in Southeastern California and*

Southwestern Nevada by W. C. Mendenhall. It states:

> Cave springs (elevation about 6,290 feet) are a well-known stopping place on the road from Daggett to Death Valley, and the water here is the last to be had before going down into the valley. The springs are near the summit of the Avawatz Mountains, and as their name indicates, they are found in large grottos or caves. As all travelers stop here, the majority of them camping over night, the place is clearly marked by camp litter. There are two springs, each about 5 feet across and each containing about 5 feet of water. They have been cleaned out and boarded up, but are not provided with a pump. The water is excellent.

The book was published in 1983. However, when I was there in 1967, there was no litter and it wasn't boarded up, but the water was surely excellent.

For years after that, when partying with friends, I often took center-stage by kind-of performing my Death Valley story. My story came to the attention of Leroy, my friend in chapter one who was murdered. Leroy knew both my dad and old Bob and was aware of their gold mine venture.

My mom hired a bail bondsman to get me out of jail. During their conversation, she told him about the gold mine and the part I'd played in it. When I was released, I performed the story for him. He said that he wouldn't charge me anything for the bond if I took him up to the mine.

It was five years since my near death experience, so I wasn't opposed to going up there again. Surprisingly, I remembered how to get there. While walking up the mountain, the bondsman kept picking up stones and making comments like, "Good color," or "I can already see the possibilities up here."

Once we were at the top I showed him the hole, and then we started back down the mountain. He told me he'd keep in touch, and when he was ready, he'd contact me and we'd stake a claim and start working it. Unfortunately, the *puer aeternus* in me wasn't stable enough to hang around waiting for him to get ready. I had some serious partying to do. I don't know if he ever called or not. Perhaps he just forgot about it, or for all I know, he went back up there on his own and became rich from it.

In 1975 Leroy contacted me in Las Vegas and asked if I was interested in going back to the mine. He said that he'd finance the whole trip. I said I would. Leroy and his friend Randy showed up one summer day in Leroy's Jeep. Randy is my friend Roger's younger brother, whom I mentioned in chapter one. Leroy's Jeep was fully loaded when they showed up, so I tossed in my pillow and sleeping bag and off we went. We stopped in Baker, gassed up, and then took off on highway 127 until we turned onto the dirt road that Skip was supposed to pick me up on. The rest of this trip is a comedy of errors.

It had been a few years since I'd been there with the bail bondsman, and I was sure that I still knew the way. I brought some Xanex, but both Leroy and Randy declined when I offered them some. Randy wasn't an addict and Leroy was in recovery. We arrived at the wash and turned left. The terrain was as hard-going as ever, but for some reason I wasn't sure that we were on the right wash. After an hour or so I admitted that we turned too soon, so we returned to the old Death Valley road. Soon I saw the entrance to the wash a couple miles farther. Again, up the wash we went. Every so often, Leroy or Randy would ask, "Richard (my nickname was Little Richard), do you recognize anything?"

"Of course I do. This is the wash."

"That's what you said last time."

"I know, but last time I was wrong."

Up we went. After another hour or so, I realized that we were on the wrong wash again.

"I thought you were sure, Richard?" quipped Leroy.

"You gotta realize it's been several years since I've been here, and the rains change the looks of these washes. I'm not taking you on a wild goose chase on purpose. Give me a fucking break," I said, getting as irritated as they were.

"Okay, okay," said Leroy, "let's just get on the right one before nightfall."

We went up another wash. After about five minutes Leroy asked, "Is this the right one?"

I said, "Yes, this is the right one."

"How do you know?" asked Randy.

"Because I recognize the way the side of the wash is over there."

"I hope you're sure," said Leroy, "because we're burning daylight."

"I'll tell you what, I'll suck both your dicks if I'm wrong!"

They laughed and then Randy looked over at Leroy and said, "I hope we're on the wrong wash."

"Yeah, me too."

About ten minutes later, I said, "Hey guys, I think we're on the wrong wash."

Leroy stopped the Jeep and both of them turned around and glared at me.

"Sorry guys, no blowjob today. I have a headache."

We went up another wrong wash, and I was again so sure that I promised more blowjobs. Finally, we were on the right wash. I said, "Hey, this is it, guys. I'll give you a blowjob right now if I'm wrong."

"You already owe us three. We're not convinced. How about the blowjob first, and then we find out if it's really the right one."

"We've already found out. I recognize that V-shaped rock over there. That's where I pulled my t-shirt over my arms and slept."

We'd passed the old car body without my noticing it. Leroy and Randy, however, were finally convinced when we came upon Cave Springs. It looked the same as when I was there in '67. We hung out for awhile and then went back down and made camp at the old car body. While we were camped I said, "Leroy, did you know that this is the only mountain range west of the Mississippi River where there are fire flies—you know, lightning bugs?"

"No shit?"

"Yeah, it has something to do with what they feed on, and this is the only place in the west where they can survive."

I could tell by the expression on his face that Randy didn't believe a word of it, and that's when I needed to turn my head to keep Leroy from seeing my face.

Randy joined in on the ruse: "Richard, aren't they only in this part of the mountain range though?"

"Yeah, there's nowhere in this mountain range where the elevation is the same as it is around here."

"How come I can't see any now?" asked Leroy.

"Because it's too early."

Around midnight, I got up to piss and Leroy asked, "What are you doing?"

"I'm taking a fucking piss, dick breath, if it's okay with you."

"What's all the commotion about?" asked Randy.

"Oh nothin'. It's just Leroy looking for fire flies," I said.

"Hey Richard, how come I still don't see any?"

I started to answer when Randy started laughing.

“Why you fuckin little liar,” said Leroy. “I didn’t believe you anyway.”

“Oh yes you did,” said Randy.

The following morning we made it to where the old trailer was, but most of it was strung all over the area from all the storms and flooding so common up there. We started walking up the mountain, and when we made it to the top I showed them where the hole was. Because this was just a scouting trip, we started back down the mountain with the intention of coming back later with more equipment. I almost didn’t make it back down the mountain because I was so out of shape. Leroy and Randy, however, were black belts in Kung Fu and were in excellent condition. I was a pitiful wreck compared to them, and they teased me unmercifully about being so out of shape.

The outcome of this part of the gold mine story is a government roadblock. The army at Ft. Irwin took issue with anyone trespassing on government property, especially gold diggers; therefore, we were unable to stake a claim. Leroy said he’d work on a loophole but his short-lived bout with staying off drugs discontinued all of his well-meaning plans for gold mining.

Had I not taken Dexies that morning, I probably would’ve waited on the dirt road for Skip to show up instead of taking off half-cocked and wired on amphetamines. Had I waited, the old man would’ve caught up with me, and neither of us would’ve been through such a harrowing ordeal.

CHAPTER NINE

Scumbags and Road Trips

Minneola Mobil is five miles north of Yermo on the way to Vegas. It's been abandoned for years, but it's still visible when passing the Minneola Road exit on I-15. My dad had a '55 Ford pick-up that he let me use to go to work and back. Meanwhile he was having the motor rebuilt in my 48 Chevy. Regardless of all the trouble I'd gotten into in my life, I still managed to retain a relatively good relationship with my parents. My dad and I had many talks together on his security patrol. Sometimes my mom went too. She and I alternated tagging doors. While we were on patrol one night I told my dad about the fraudulent sales practices going on at Minneola Mobil. He was as intrigued as I was. What I didn't tell him was the easy money I was making with my own version of fraudulent sales practices.

The guys I worked with were salesmen called fifty-percenters (50%ers), because their only income was fifty percent of the profit from what they sold, while the other fifty percent went to the station owner. The owners of these types of stations were known as merchandisers. Later I became a 50%er myself, but at this time, I was content with stealing gas caps.

Walking up to a customer's window I said, "Hello, can I help you?"

"Yes, fill it up with super please."

When I took off their gas cap, I slipped it into my pocket, returned to the window and said, "You don't have a gas cap, sir."

"What! Oh, that idiot back in Vegas must have forgotten to put it back on. Do you have one?"

"I'll go check, sir." While the gas was still running, I left as though I was checking, then came back and sold them their own gas cap. Occasionally, people wouldn't buy one, so I accumulated a collection of them so I wouldn't have to sell them back their own: there was always the chance they'd recognize it. Selling 10 to 15 gas caps a shift at two or three dollars apiece came in handy for my insatiable appetite for drugs and alcohol.

Sometime between my arrest in August and my surrender to do the time in December of '67 for drunk in public and resisting arrest, Minneola Mobil went out of business. Merchandisers made a lot of money while they were in business, but often they didn't last long because of customer complaints.

My old Chevy was back on the road, so Crazy Clyde and I went to visit some friends in Chino, CA. I'm still asking myself why I continued to hang out with that lying, thieving, scumbag.

After partying all night, we spent the night in the back room of our friend's head shop. Early the next morning, I woke up with Clyde shaking my arm and saying, "Let's go, c'mon, let's go—hurry up."

"What?" I said wiping the sleep out of my eyes.

"We gotta go," said Clyde hurriedly, "C'mon. Now! Get up."

"Okay, okay, what's your fucking hurry?"

"I'll tell you later. C'mon, let's go."

Once we were on the road I asked, "Okay Clyde, what's this all about?"

"Someone came to the door and told me the place was about to be busted."

"Then why didn't you tell Paul and Vic and everybody else?" I asked.

"There wasn't time. It's better that some of us get away than none of us.

Why I accepted his explanation, I don't know, but I'm sure I was skeptical. However, I found out on the way to Tijuana when my car broke down. I needed to get into the trunk for my wallet because it was still in my dirty pants, but before I reached the trunk, Clyde said, "Wait! Don't get in there."

"Huh? What do you mean, don't get in there?

Clyde couldn't think of a reason, so he said, "Trust me, don't get in there. C'mon, I'll tell you about it later."

"Trust you?" I asked as I put the key in and laughed, "Who in the fuck would trust you?" As soon as I lifted the trunk, I knew. There was our friends' stereo equipment, plus a couple musical instruments and an amplifier.

"You lying, thieving, scumbag fucking sewer rat!"

"It ain't what you think," replied Clyde as he raised his hands in defense.

"The fuck it ain't!"

"I didn't do it, Little Richard, swear to God."

"Don't piss on my back and try to tell me I'm sweating."

Clyde replied first with his muffled laugh, "Ha ha ha ha," then said, "Richard, I can explain."

I was pissed. We could never go back there again, unless we returned the equipment, but we couldn't do that because we were stranded. Finally I said, "Shut up, Clyde. There ain't a fucking thing you can say that I'll believe. We'll just leave the car here for the time being and hitchhike the rest of the way. We'll worry about it when we leave T.J."

Clyde said, "Okay, let's go," and stuck his thumb out.

When we arrived in T.J., we rented a cheap room and then went to a bar where each of us bought a whore. When we finished our business, we bought some whites on a street corner to get wired. Then we bought some reds to bring us down and then more whites. We alternated back and forth with the reds and whites, and eventually we were separated. I couldn't remember where our room was, so I continued my drug-crazed vigil by myself.

I was alone and in an incoherent state of mind. Whenever I ran out of money I started panhandling, telling people that I just needed money enough for a phone call. I passed out for a while in a bar and when I awoke my wallet was gone. I was a mess, but I wanted to continue partying. It was a weekend, and there were still plenty of people on the street, so it didn't take me long to panhandle enough money to go back into the bars and drink it up some more. Then I'd go out and panhandle some more. Again, I'd get some whites and get wired, and then some reds to take the edge off. About five o'clock in the morning the people on the streets were thinning out and I started hitting on some of the same people. I started hearing responses like, "Think of a new line, pal, this one's getting old," or, "No way, asshole, you told us the same thing an hour ago." It was time to leave the dirty city.

At the edge of town I ran into two brothers I went to high school with. "Hey Carl, Ronnie!" I yelled as I started toward them.

When they turned around, Carl said jokingly, "Little Richard, where's your taxi? I heard you was living down here." Carl was joking, but I wasn't in a joking mood.

"Actually," I replied, "I'm not doing so well."

Then Ronnie asked, "What's wrong with you? You look rummy."

I gave them a hard-luck story and asked for a loan. They gave it to me but instead of using the money to get home, I turned around and went back to the streets downtown and started partying it up again—doing the same things I'd been doing all day and the night before.

When I finally crossed the border back into the U.S., I went to where Crazy Clyde and I left the car, but it wasn't there. I found out that the police didn't have it either, so I assumed that Clyde ditched me in Tijuana and came back and stole it. At this point, I even suspected him of rigging it so it would break down.

Goddamn that dirty fucking Clyde! God damn me for hanging out with him. He'd steal the gold out of his mother's mouth. That bastard really would.

To this day I believe he stole my car, and then sold it in Tijuana. I believe this scenario because my dad later received a letter from someone in Tijuana asking for the title.

I walked a couple blocks and saw a big lawn and some shade trees, so I went there and layed down. I woke up to a police officer shaking me. Once I was awake, he asked me for my I.D. I didn't have one so I told him about it being stolen in Tijuana. He told me I was under arrest for investigation of burglary, and then he cuffed me. On the way to the jail in San Diego, I asked, "I'm not really under arrest for suspicion of burglary, am I?" You just want to detain me long enough to find out who I am and if I have any warrants."

I remember his exact words: "Yeah, something like that."

I called my mom and ask her to send me twenty dollars because I knew I'd be released without formal charges being filed. Forty-eight hours later, when I was released for a lack of evidence, there was twenty dollars on my books, and there was also, forever and always, an arrest on my police record for investigation of burglary. Instead of using the money to get home on, I went back to Tijuana and did it all over again for two more days. It wasn't long before I was supposed to turn myself in for the 60 days I had to do in the county jail, which was my reason for partying so hard.

Not long after the gold mine debacle, I met Bonnie, one of my most memorable girlfriends. Our relationship started as a strictly sexual one—at least for me. Whenever I felt the urge, I'd call her. If she were at home and was inclined, we'd both walk to the nearest motel. Bonnie and I were young with voracious sexual appetites, so when I didn't have the money for a motel, we'd enjoy each other wherever we could. Bonnie was a looker, but I wasn't yet ready to settle down, and it was my assumption that she wasn't either. When I think about her, however, I believe my assumption might have been wrong. I don't know. A *puer*, as I stated before, is continually in and out of romantic relationships.

The night before I turned myself in, I wanted to get laid, so I called Bonnie. Fortunately, she was home and in the mood. We met at a motel and spent the night together. When we left the motel room the next morning, she walked home, and I hitchhiked to Berdoo to surrender.

While I was at Camp Snoopy, my dad was involved in a car accident. His leg was amputated and he was given a 50/50 chance to live. He was 67 years and not very healthy. My mom did everything she could to get me released temporarily to go to his bedside, but to no avail. Fortunately, he didn't die while I was locked up.

Not long after my release from Camp Snoopy, I was at home when the telephone rang. To my delight, it was my childhood sweetheart, Lynda. She said she was downtown and getting ready to walk to my house. I told her I too would start walking and meet her in the middle. On my way, I ran into a guy I knew. He said, "Hey Richard, check out that fox walking up the street."

With boastful pride I said, "I intend to. She's coming here to meet me."

Wow! I see what he means. What a knock out! She still looks 17. Lynda was two years older than me, which made her 24 at the time. While her youthful appearance served her well most of the time, it also worked against her when we'd try to patronize nightclubs and bars. Because she didn't drive, she didn't have a license to use for identification. Looking young for her age was still a nuisance to her when she was 28 years old.

After she stayed with me for a few days we decided to live together. My dad was bedridden from his accident and she comforted him while she was there, but it wasn't long before he was back in the hospital. He was also being fitted with a prosthetic leg, and eventually his condition appeared to be improving.

Lynda and I lived at different apartments around town, but when we were living at my parents' house, I landed a job driving a cab. Desert Ambulance

Service was in the same building and run by the same people, so they shared the same radio frequency. One day I heard on my cab's radio that an ambulance was being dispatched to my house, so I arrived there about the same time the ambulance did. Lynda had attempted suicide. She tried to overdose on reds as well as cutting her wrist. It was a bloody mess. My mom was beside herself and so was I.

My parents didn't want us living there anymore. Who could blame them? My mom loved Lynda, especially when she was a young girl, but now she had emotional problems that my mom was incapable of dealing with any longer, so we moved.

My parents owned a '65 Plymouth Valiant that they let Lynda and me have. My dad was back in the hospital at Loma Linda, and his prognosis wasn't good. My mom spent time with him for a while, but she couldn't stay because she needed to coordinate the work schedules of the security officers who worked for my dad. One of them was my friend Larry's father. Lynda and I also spent time at the hospital, so we traded off as much as possible.

Lynda and I slept in the hospital parking lot. One evening I went to my dad's room to visit for a while, but he was having trouble staying awake. A doctor took me aside and said, "He's just been given 50 milligrams of Seconal, so you should probably let him get some rest." I said okay, but as I was walking out of his hospital room, I thought I saw something in his demeanor that was beckoning me back, but it was so subtle that I ignored it and returned to the car to join Lynda.

Sometime during the night I awoke and sat straight up with my eyes wide open. I remember looking up toward my dad's room and then going to sleep again. When I awoke in the morning, I went to his room. As I was passing the nurses station, one of them stopped me and said, "I'm sorry sir, but your dad passed away during the night."

Did I wake up at the same time that he died? I wondered. I didn't check the time, but I was then, and have since been convinced that those two events were synchronous. The bond between us was broken while we were both in an unconscious state, and I believe that severance woke me up. I went into the room and stood by his bed. His face was so serene and peaceful compared to the pain, exhaustion, and struggle of the day before. I then understood what is meant by,

"He is at peace now." The contrast was so visible.

I went back to the car and told Lynda. I guess I said it so matter-of-factly that she said, "You don't seem very upset."

"I guess I'm in shock. He's always been there. Although I know I'll never see him again, I don't feel like it's real." I didn't cry. I didn't even cry when I was alone. My relationship with Lynda demanded all of my emotional stamina. I was so preoccupied with her that I didn't have time to grieve. My dad and I were close. There might have been a generation gap or two between us, but we were still close, and I loved him as much as any son could love his father. I was really lucky to have a father like him. I revere him today and have for many years, but as a self-centered 23-year-old drug and alcohol addict on an emotional roller coaster with an emotionally unbalanced woman, I just wasn't capable of grieving, I literally repressed my dad's death.

CHAPTER TEN

Counterfeiting and Smuggling

Lynda and I were visiting my mom when my aunt and uncle showed up with their youngest son. My cousin, Jimmy, was the closest to my age among his brother and sisters. After some small talk, he made an excuse for us to leave and we started cruising around in his parents' car. "Johnny," he asked, "do you know where I can pass a couple counterfeit twenty dollar bills?"

"Hmm, I suppose you'd prefer small businesses?"

"Yeah, kinda out of the way."

"Okay, turn around and go back the other direction. I'll take you to the little bar and grill where our uncle Orvil spent many drunken hours."

After discussing the drunken antics of our bibulous uncle for a couple miles, we parked next to the Greystone Cafe. While Jimmy was getting ready to go in, I said, "Let me see one of those bills."

As he was reaching for his wallet, he said, "The printing is perfect, but they look like they've been bleached."

"Yeah, and they... they look new and crisp."

Then he took it out of my hand and wadded it up and rolled it around in his hands and said, "Yeah... that's why I do this." Before he went into the store, he asked, "Want a beer?"

"Yeah, I'll take a Bud."

When he returned, he set a six pack between us and asked, "How about another place?"

I said, "Okay," and took him to a market in Lenwood and to another in a little rural community called Grandview. After finishing our six-pack and passing three bogus twenties, we returned to the house and resumed our visit.

During that time I pumped gas in various service stations around town: While working at an American station, Larry, the friend I worked with when Hickey died, was working at the Mobil just up the street. He and I wanted to make extra money, so we pooled our next paychecks and bought a kilo of pot. After paying a hundred dollars for it, we took it to Larry's apartment, broke it up and put it into baggies to sell.

We learned there was someone else in town selling a lot of pot, which was keeping us from selling ours as fast. We found out who it was, but neither of us knew him. One day while getting high at his apartment, Larry said, "We should start dealing in kilos instead of cans." We still called them cans from the days when they were commonly sold in Prince Albert tobacco cans.

"I guess we'll have to build up to it," I said

"That'll take too long."

Then I had a revelation: "Well then," I said with a pompous smile, "I guess we're just gonna have to go into the counterfeit money business."

"Huh? What are you talking about?" Larry asked.

I then told him about my cousin. Although the counterfeit twenties made the local paper after my cousin left, a couple months had gone by. Once we sold most of the lids (another word for cans) from the kilo, I called my cousin.

"Hello."

"Jimmy, how's it going?"

"I can't complain, and you?"

"Good," I replied, "I was wondering if you can still get those counterfeit twenties?"

"Yeah."

"How much?"

"It'll cost ya seven dollars for each twenty."

"How soon can I come and get em?"

"Whenever you want."

Larry and I split the profits from slinging pot, kept aside some operating money, and went to Monterey Park to invest $400. That gave us each $560 in counterfeit twenties. We split up the funny money, went back to Barstow, and set out on separate paths to earn our respective profits. I drove south and passed all of mine at little mom and pop markets and small cafes between Lucerne Valley and Victorville on highway 18, usually buying a six-pack or a snack. Larry drove east and passed all of his at similar places between Barstow and Needles on old highway 66. By the time each of us had passed 30 counterfeit twenties, we had somewhere around $600 apiece after expenses.

We then had investment capital. We learned through the grapevine that the pot dealer who kept us from selling ours fast enough, worked at Denny's as a cook. Larry and I took a friend who knew him to Denny's so we could be introduced. When he came out of the back door of the restaurant, Andy said, "JD, this is Little Richard and Larry. I'm sure you've heard of them."

"I have," replied JD as he stuck out his hand.

After introductions, Larry said, "You put a damper on our pot sales for awhile JD, so we thought if we pooled our resources, we could all make money without stepping on each other's toes."

"What do you have in mind?"

"Well," said Larry, "that depends on how much you can get kilos for."

JD thought for a minute and said, "thirty-five dollars."

"That's a good price," I said.

"Yeah," agreed Larry. "You see JD, we've been paying a hundred, so here's our offer: since you have the connection, we'll pay for it, and then we'll split the profit three ways."

"Listen," said JD, "I'm interested, but right now I have to get back inside. Why don't you come by and pick me up when I get off at eleven, and we'll talk some more."

Later, when discussing our proposal, we discovered that JD was smuggling kilos of marijuana out of Tijuana. That's why his buying price was so low. By our standards, JD was funny looking. He wore thick horned-rimmed glasses and was baldheaded, making him look like a nerd

After more discussion and some negotiating, we went into the drug-smuggling business with JD. Neither of us cared much for JD's dry and impersonal disposition, so we didn't really try to be friends with him. This was business. We all agreed that it was not necessary for all three of us to go to Tijuana, so JD rented a car and he and I made the trip.

Once we crossed the border and drove through the downtown area where the street-corner whores, nightclubs, and crazy taxi drivers were, we entered a sleazy, rancid-smelling area with pot-holed pavement and dirt roads. We ended up in an alley next to a dingy-looking tenement building.

I waited in the car. Out of my view, JD gave his connection $1,000 for 28 kilos of pot. After making the transaction, JD motioned for me to bring over the car. We transferred the pot from an empty apartment to the trunk of the car. I never saw JD's pot connection. On the way back to the border, we began feeling the inevitable fear that balled up in the middle of our stomachs. Being jailed in Tijuana for a large-scale smuggling beef was a frightening thought, so JD proceeded carefully.

Then something happened. A cop was standing on a corner just as we reentered the downtown area and was looking straight at us. Right away JD noticed the panic welling up in me as we were approaching the stop sign. He said, "Don't even think about jumping out of the car and making a run for it." Once I told him that I wasn't that stupid, JD slowly edged the car ahead until we were out of sight of the cop. He probably wasn't even looking at us.

"That scared the shit out of me, JD."

"I can see that."

"Well, there's really no sense in both of us crossing the border."

With a jaundiced eye, he replied, "What do you mean?"

"Let me ask you something. How many times have you done this?"

"Five or six times, but you have to realize that I haven't *ever* smuggled across this much."

"That's my point, you've done it several times, but I've *never* done it, and you just saw how I react to cops."

"Yeah, worrying about what you were going to do back there was worse than worrying about the damn cop."

"That's what I mean, JD. Do you really want to take that chance with me in the car? Besides, doesn't it make more sense for one of us to get busted than both of us?"

"Richard, are you just trying to get out of crossing the border?"

"Of course I am, but it makes sense. If we both get busted, who's going to get us out? If you alone get busted, I can get back to Barstow and Larry and I can both work on bailing you out and getting a lawyer. With both of us locked up, we might not be able to reach Larry or anyone else.

"That does make sense," JD said, "so why don't you drive the car across and if you get busted, I can do all that?"

"Because, you just proved that you work better under pressure than I do. Besides, the car is rented in your name, and you've done this several times before."

We finally agreed by the time I got out to walk across the border; however, JD entered another fearful phase—crossing the border with 28 kilos of pot in the trunk of the car.

I started walking toward the border as JD drove away. Twenty minutes later I reached the Jack in the Box on the U.S. side of the border. Then, I started sweating bullets while I waited for JD. *Shit! I've been here for ten minutes. What's taking so fucking long? He's busted, I know it. Fuck, now what?* After all this panic went on for what seemed like an interminable amount of time, JD finally pulled into the driveway. I jumped into the car, hit him on the shoulder, and said, "Right on JD ole boy, we did it!"

"Yeah, I did it," JD said solemnly while giving me the evil eye.

He and I made another trip to Tijuana, repeating what we did the first time, minus all the panic. After that we started living the good life. We had a bunch of money with more owed to us, but we were greedy. We decided to make just one more trip by car, and then we were going to research other modes of smuggling.

We rented a big fancy apartment in Bell Gardens, near LA, so we could be more centrally located for the majority of our customers. Larry and JD each had his own bedroom, and Lynda and I had the third bedroom. We all agreed that Lynda's role in the operation, at first anyway, would be that of cook and housekeeper.

We eventually came to the conclusion that Lynda could be of help. Having her in the car with JD when he crossed the border would cause less suspicion. Since this was going to be our last trip in a car, we wanted to reduce as much as possible the chances of getting caught. The three of us made the trip, and as usual, I left the car just before the border.

When JD and Lynda were waiting in the long line of cars to cross back into the states with all the pot, Lynda started to panic: "JD, I'm scared."

"Lynda, I've done this a lot, so try to be calm." About that time JD started to put a cigarette out in the ashtray, but he accidentally dropped it on the floor.

"Be calm, huh? Then why in the fuck are you shaking like a whore in church?"

"Just get that cigarette before the carpet catches on fire," JD said calmly.

Just as I was showing my I.D. at the border as a pedestrian, I saw a bunch of immigration officers running out of the building and over to the car that JD and Lynda were crossing in. The officer looked at me and said, "Looks like they found another load of dope," then he handed back my I.D., and I walked safely across the border

Oh shit! What am I going to do now? Damn! I need help. This wasn't supposed to happen. Why didn't it happen before Lynda was involved. Ohhh, no. My poor Lynda. She didn't ask for all this. What am I going to do? She'll probably hate me after this. I'll probably lose her.

By the time I made it to the Jack in the Box, I was an emotional basket case, and this time, JD wouldn't be showing up. He and my girlfriend were in jail for smuggling—a federal offense. I went inside and bought a coke. *Damn! I need something stronger than this, but I don't see any bars or liquor stores around here. I could go find one. No way, I gotta keep my head on straight. Oh, I wonder... I wonder if Billy still lives in Escondido. Hmm.*

Because Escondido wasn't too far away, I called the number I had for Billy on a pay phone. He was there, and he immediately came to pick me up. After explaining what happened, it was obvious that I needed financial help, and he was fortunately in a position to accommodate me.

Billy was in possession of a large amount of heroin, and what worked in my favor, was that he wasn't strung out yet. In good faith he fronted me a considerable amount of it. We both fixed, but I didn't use any more after that, because it still didn't set well with my stomach. Billy and his girlfriend gave me a ride back to Barstow, trusting and believing my promise to pay him back once we sold the heroin. If I'd been an active heroin addict, he wouldn't have been so trusting, nor would he have been paid back.

Larry and I both used heroin periodically over the years, but I managed to avoid a habit because of my intolerance to it. Still, we both knew many addicts in the high desert, people we had bought and sold drugs to before. Between the smaller quantities of pot that we had delegated to sell, and the heroin we sold, we were in a financial position to bail Lynda out and of jail and hire a lawyer for her; however, we were forced to give up our apartment in Bell Gardens.

What happened to JD? Well, we just left him in jail. He'd served his purpose so he ended up being a pawn in a relationship that was strictly business. It all seemed so justified, especially considering JD's dry and boring personality; in fact, we even thought of him as an asshole. But that wasn't the last Lynda and I saw of him. JD bailed out too and when Lynda and I drove to San Diego for court appearances, we often saw him there. He wouldn't talk to us, however, and I couldn't blame him.

The lawyer we hired for Lynda didn't work out, so like JD, we went with a public defender who took a more aggressive stand. I told the PD everything—about our operation and my two accomplices. He said, "Oh, I see. Lynda here was just a window dresser?"

"That's right," I replied, even though I'd never heard that term before. Lynda and I made several trips to San Diego before the case was resolved. She was finally convicted of some misdemeanor charge and given summary probation. Once we paid Billy back for the heroin and collected the rest of what was owed to us, the chapter of my life as a counterfeiter, drug smuggling drug dealer was over.

CHAPTER ELEVEN

The Trickster as Lube Bay Bandit

When Lynda was first pregnant with our daughter, we moved to South San Gabriel, and I found a job at a Holiday Inn in the industrial district of Montebello as a bell-hop. The clientele was mostly businessmen; therefore, I made about three to six dollars a day in tips. At first, that was enough to keep us in food and gas, and me in vodka. Lynda remained abstinent during her pregnancy but she didn't mind that I drank a half-pint every evening after work. Unfortunately I was caught trying to sleep away a hangover in one of the rooms and was fired.

In those days there were two types of service stations—the tourist traps (merchandizers) such as Minneola Mobil where I stole gas caps, and the local stations that catered to the community. I landed a job in a local station in San Gabriel; therefore, I couldn't get away with stealing gas caps, so I was forced to stay honest. I was accustomed to daily tips at the Holiday Inn. They sustained us between paychecks, but after being fired, that luxury was gone, so I needed to find another source of daily income for vodka and other necessities; therefore, I invented a scam. I'm probably not the only one who came up with the idea, but it was my brainchild in that I didn't learn it from someone else. I went to super market parking lots and picked up receipts that other customers had discarded. When I found one with an item purchased for five dollars or more, I went into the store, and found an item that matched the price on the receipt, and then turned it in for a refund. This would be impossible with the more sophisticated cash registers of today.

Baby Lynda was born on May 13, 1969. Lynda had convinced me that she didn't need prenatal care because she'd already given birth to three children from her first marriage. I didn't know any better, so I didn't insist. The first time I saw my daughter, she was in an incubator and screaming so vehemently that her little veins were bulging out of her head. I said to my cousin Sonny "Wow, she's quite the sniveler for only weighing three pounds and 15 ounces." From that moment her nickname was Snivels until she was around 12 when it became an embarrassment to her.

My old friend Huck moved in with us. His wife in New Mexico kicked him out because of his obsession with drugs and alcohol. Naturally he and I started drinking and using and staying out too much. When Huck and I came home from a bar one night, Lynda and Snivels were gone.

It wasn't long before Lynda and I and Snivels reconciled. Huck returned to New Mexico to his family, and I found a job at another local station, this time in Wilmar, CA. We resumed life as we knew it before Huck moved in, but a major change was just around the corner.

My friend Gimmy and his wife, Dee, showed up for a visit. Noticing our low-income living conditions, Gimmy suggested we come to Newhall for a visit and see how well they were doing. A couple weeks later, we visited them on my days off, and I was indeed impressed with their big house and nice furniture. Gimmy introduced me to his boss (a merchandiser like Minneola Mobil). The owner of the station ended up financing my move to Newhall, where I'd be trained as a salesman, selling tires, shocks, and fuel pumps. This merchandiser would not hire 50%ers because they had the reputation as being undependable or drifty. Because 50%ers worked on straight commission, they only worked when they wanted to. Our boss, whom I'll refer to as Gypper1, paid us a monthly salary but we'd have to work 10 hours a day, six days a week for it. In addition to our salaries, he paid us five dollars a unit—a unit being a shock, tire, or fuel pump. If we sold 10 units on our shift, we were paid a ten-dollar bonus in addition to our $50.00 in commission. Business was good, so it wasn't unusual for salesmen to sell 10 to 20 units every day.

Thus began my career as a service station salesman, and later as one of those drifty 50%ers who worked only when they wanted to. On a typical day a motorist would pull onto the island of a major brand service station to fill with gas. I approached the customer with a smile and asked, "What can I do for you today, sir?"

"Fill it up with super," replied the customer, taking in the familiar smell of gasoline and the musky odor of rain.

At a time when long hair and beards were cool, I wore short hair and was clean-shaven. I was courteous and I looked sharp in my clean white station shirt and trousers. I eagerly did as the customer asked. Once the gas was started, sometimes I returned to the car window and asked the customer if he or she'd like me to check under the hood. Most of the time, however, I wouldn't ask, I just lifted the hood as though they expected it of me.

It was characteristic to see a red grease-rag in a salesman's hand or hanging out of his hip pocket. I carried mine in my hand when I approached a customer. Inside of it, I carried a small Elmer's Glue bottle filled with hydraulic fluid that I'd previously extracted from an old shock absorber. It took me only a few seconds to bend down, reach under the car, and squirt a little of the fluid on one of the front shocks while the hood was up.

"Excuse me sir," I said—no longer smiling, "you have oil leaking under your car."

"Oil? Where is it coming from?"

"I can't tell for sure, but it's dreadfully close to your tire, sir. Just in case it's brake fluid or something, maybe we should pull it into the lube bay. It won't cost you anything to put it on the rack and check it, and it could save you trouble on the road."

"Okay, if you don't mind."

What occurred between me and the unwitting customer was a confidence game. Off ramps on Interstates was where merchandisers usually set up shop. Tourists were the ones that were at the mercy of highway robbers like us. Local customers, such as the ones who patronized the stations in San Gabriel or Wilmar, usually took their vehicles to their own mechanics, so we avoided locals. However, when it came to tourists, the motto of the merchandiser was *kill'em with kindness but be heartless in the pursuit of the sale*.

Once the car was on the rack, I pointed out to the customer that the seal on the front shock absorber had ruptured and was leaking fluid. "To save yourself a much higher repair bill later, sir, you should replace these shocks now. It doesn't matter where you buy them. You can get them at a part's store and install them yourself, or you can buy them at a department store where they're less expensive.

However you decide to do it, you'll be money ahead in the long run doing it prior to any further damage." Then I'd explain what could happen to their vehicle if they continued to drive with damaged shocks.

"Do you sell shocks here?"

"Yes we do."

"How much does it cost and how long does it take?"

I quoted a price and told them that I could complete the installation within fifteen minutes. "Furthermore, sir, this merchandise is guaranteed for the life of your car—anywhere in the United States or Canada, as long as it's at one of our stations." This professional con job usually cost the customer hundreds, if not thousands of dollars.

"Okay, put em on."

While the customer waited, he listened to the deafening roar of the impact wrench, parts dropping on the floor, and traffic driving by outside. When the fifteen minutes were almost up, I walked into the waiting area where the customer was patiently waiting and said, "Sir, would you come with me, please?"

I brought the customer under the upraised car and pointed to one of the rear shocks. "Looky here, sir, this rear shock isn't quite as bad as the front one, but the leaking has started here too. The truth is, you could probably go awhile before any real damage is done back here, but to be on the safe side, it's only an additional fifteen minutes to install these." During my spiel, the customer sensed honesty and concern, so he agreed.

While I was installing shocks, I evaluated the condition of the customer's tires. If the car was fairly new and the tires had less than six or eight thirty-seconds of rubber on them and the owners had a credit card, then they were also prime targets for a tire sale. Flaws and defects can easily be found on most tires, which can be exaggerated; however, why take the chance that the customer might not buy tires? Therefore, to insure they would, we salesmen carried a small, sharpened, stubby screwdriver, called a honker, which was used to cut the tire a little—just enough to show the cords on the inside of the sidewall or between the tread. I did this to two or three of the tires and the result was generally the sale of a set of new tires.

Another approach to selling tires was on the island when motorists were gassing up. If I noticed that a customer's car already had new shocks, then I'd go for something else. In my shirt pocket, I carried another devious little tool called a pinner. It was also a small screwdriver but not the stubby kind. This little screwdriver was sharpened to poke small holes in tires. I wouldn't pin a tire on the island while they were gassing up, because if they didn't take their cars into the lube bay, then they'd leave and have a flat down the road. Some salesmen had a conscience, but many did not. After checking under the hood, I grabbed an air hose and pretended to air up their front tire. As I was doing this, I looked up at the customer and told her that her tire only had about 10 or 15 pounds of air in it, a condition that was cause for alarm. I offered to pull the car into the lube bay and check it. I told the customer that if there wasn't anything wrong with the tire, he could safely go on his way at no charge. If there was, then it would cost to repair or replace the tire. While I was adjusting the racks, I'd pin the one that I'd low-tired on the island, and then honk two or three of the others.

Depending on how convinced and how willing customers were to part with their money determined whether I'd continue to sell them parts and accessories. Another major criteria for how far I pressed was how unscrupulous or money-hungry the owner of the station was. If the owner didn't care what lengths we went to for a sale, then the sky was the limit and we continued to drain customers. However, if the owner wanted to stay in business, then he needed to make an effort to avoid customer complaints, therefore deceitful or fraudulent sales tactics would be limited or prohibited. By the time customers rolled out of the driveway, they were usually happy and grateful that the condition of their vehicle was brought to their attention and taken care of so efficiently. To break down on the highway would be undesirable; therefore, service stations and their bright and friendly attendants were sometimes thought of as *saviors of the road.*

Sometimes customers didn't have "to be sold," just the mention of something wrong would persuade the customer to repair or replace whatever the vehicle needed: "Okay, whatever you think the car needs, just put it on or fix it. We have a credit card and don't want to have any trouble on the road."

With customers so willing to part with their money, salesmen were all too willing to take it. After four shocks and a set of tires, I'd often continue replacing parts such as fan clutches, batteries, alternators, and fuel pumps. More often, however, it was one of those smaller items that I'd sell first, and then move on to more expensive parts and labor. Furthermore, merchandisers usually stocked all the parts. In the event we didn't have the parts in stock, it took only minutes to have them delivered from a local part's house, or we borrowed them from another merchandiser. In Barstow, for example, there were at least ten other merchandisers to borrow from. There were even more in the Victorville area. On the way to Vegas there were merchandisers in Baker, and of course in Las Vegas they were up and down the strip from the Alladin Hotel all the way through North Las Vegas.

Merchandisers were bilking the public all over the United States until the TV show *60 Minutes* did an expose on the practice. The expose' didn't really put a stop to it—it merely made us more astute in sizing up our prey and in our approach.

Being savagely unscrupulous was one end of the spectrum. The other end was legitimacy. When I worked on the Las Vegas strip, most of the merchandisers were questionably legitimate. I say, questionably, because deceptive sales practices were still going on. Their definition of legitimacy was for their salesmen to sell dry—that is without pinners, honkers, and squirt bottles. The result was the same, most customers left service stations having spent hundreds or thousands of dollars on merchandise that wasn't defective. Whether the customers needed the parts or not, it is a good thing that mini markets have replaced the widespread practice of the *lube bay bandits* and the tricksters who worked in them.

To be sure, by this time I'd been personifying the *puer* for several years, but when wants and/or needs start applying pressure to make more money for those wants or needs, the trickster archetype emerges. With me, trickster psychology started with gas caps and supermarket receipts, but we all have the ability to invoke that inner trickster. An archetype is a universal behavioral pattern among a multitude of patterns that are available to us if or when we need them. Sometimes, we only personify the trickster during times of financial crises, and then we often dissociate from him. With drug addicts, he becomes a permanent embodiment. My inner *puer* was still alive and well and remained with me until I was 45 years old, but when I went to work in Newhall as a lube bay bandit, the trickster also became a permanent part of my personality that endured. Those two archetypes are commonly found in criminalized drug addicts. For more information on this phenomenon, read my book *Scumbag Sewer Rats: An Archetypal Understanding of Criminalized Drug Addicts* or go to my website at www.ScumbagSewerRats.com.

A famous example of a contemporary *puer*/trickster is Frank Abagnale Jr., portrayed by Leonardo Dicaprio in *Catch Me If You Can*. Another example is in *The Thomas Crown Affair* with Pierce Brosnan. I can hardly compare myself to such brilliant examples, but my reason for mentioning them is to elucidate how versatile the trickster can be—from the lowly receipt refunder and 50%er to a world famous con artist. Most cultures have mythological trickster figures. In the Greek pantheon, it was Hermes. In Native American culture, it was the Winnebago Indian Wakdjunkaga, and in the animal kingdom it's the wily coyote. In ancient Japanese culture, it was the taboo-breaking Susa-No-O. Wherever he goes, whether in ancient times or in the future, he is a vagabond, an intruder to proper society and an unpredictable liar who throws doubt on the concept of truth itself. By breaking the patterns of a culture, the trickster helps define those patterns; by acting irresponsibly he helps define responsibility.

~

My relationship with Lynda was a rocky one, and we broke up again while we were living in Newhall. I worked for Gypper1 for a year or more and I worked in the business for about ten years. I was a 50%er for awhile on the grapevine (I-10 between Newhall and Bakersfield), and then Lynda and I reconciled and lived in Barstow again. When I was working at Gypper2's Shell station in Barstow, I met Wilder. He was also living with a woman, so Lynda and I often socialized with them. Gypper2 also owned a station in Victorville, so we all moved there to work. Lynda and I rented an apartment in neighboring Apply Valley. While I was working for Gypper2, I had an ironic experience.

I needed a battery for my truck but I didn't want to buy one—not even at the discounted price I could've gotten it for through the station, so I went to a local country club. I went to the parking lot and started lifting hoods (that was before inside hood latches) until I found an easy one to open, and then I stole the battery. The next morning I didn't have to push-start my truck, I just turned the key like a normal vehicle and drove to work. A couple hours later a middle-aged man in a suit walked up to the station and asked, "Do you sell batteries?"

"Yes sir."What kind of vehicle is it for?"

When I went to look it up, he mumbled, "Son-of-a-bitch."

I turned around and said, "Pardon me?"

"Oh, sorry. I'm just pissed off. You see, the only reason I need a battery is because some son-of-a-bitch stole the battery out of my car last night."

I started to say something to let him know that I sympathized with his anger, but when I started to speak I didn't think I could keep from laughing, so I put myself through a minor coughing fit to cover it. When I regained my composure, I said, "Damn, what kind of ass-hole would do such a thing?"

"A dirty rotten scumbag, that's who!"

"I agree, sir, only a despicable sewer rat would do that."

My unstable little family became a little more unstable when we returned home one night and found that our house had been burglarized and our color TV stolen. Lynda was beside herself with anger, blaming me, the neighbors, our friends, and then anybody that she could think of. She insisted that we move, and after arguing about the move for a week or two, I acquiesced and we moved back to the Barstow area in Grandview. I guess it had been my turn to be the recipient of some poetic justice.

During this time we went with my mom to the state prison at Tehatchapi to visit her brother. After visiting with him for a while, we learned that he was going to be released soon. He'd been locked up for 21 years for forcible rape and kidnapping, crimes that my mom insisted he didn't commit. Supposedly, it was a case of mistaken identity.

Grandview was where our common law marriage (we were married in Tijuana but it wasn't legal in the States) ended. We'd been together, off and on, for three rocky years. She moved in with our next door neighbor's son, and I moved into an apartment with my friend Porker.

Porker and I shared various apartments around Barstow that summer. I worked at another station, and he was digging ditches until he was laid off. I said, "If you're not gonna work then I ain't either," so I quit my job, which wasn't an unusual thing for me to do. Jobs for 50%ers were plentiful enough that I could go to work just about any place or anytime I wanted. Moreover, there were always unemployment benefits. We both stayed unemployed until our unemployment benefits were exhausted. That summer was a memorable one, in that we survived on very little food and an inordinate amount of alcohol.

I moved in with Iggy Willy for a short time in Las Vegas. There were plenty of merchandisers there, so getting jobs wasn't a problem. I talked to the manager of a Gulf station in North Las Vegas. Gypper3 said he couldn't pay me a salary, and I said fifty-percent would be fine. In the first hour of my first day, I sold a *four and four*, which meant four tires and four shocks to the same customer. From then on, I could do no wrong in Gypper3's eyes. He thought I was slicker than two snakes swimming in a barrel of snot, but really, it was the luck of the draw, with the draw being the right customers coming into the right station, at the right times with the right salesman waiting on them.

An elderly lady pulled into the station one day. Bananas, another salesman, lured her into the lube bay. Once inside, he said, "Ma'am, you can stay in the car while I raise it up if you like."

"Is it safe?"

"Absolutely, ma'am. There's no sense waiting in that hot waiting room where there's no air conditioning. Besides it won't take that long."

After a few minutes he came to the driver side of the vehicle, looked up and said, "Ma'am, you need four new tires."

"Oh mercy," she said, "I can't afford that."

"Do you have a credit card?"

"Well... yes, but..."

That's all Bananas needed to hear. He cut her off by saying, "Ma'am, in good conscience, I cannot allow you to drive away from here with tires in that condition. It would be endangering your life and the lives of others on the highway."

What it amounted to, Bananas wouldn't let her down until she bought a full set of tires. Obviously, Gypper3 didn't mind what lengths his salesmen went to for sales. Before Bananas was finished with her, he also sold her four new shocks, upper and lower ball joints, an idler arm, and a transmission overhaul. The bill was astronomical. Fortunately, he didn't keep her in the uplifted car during the whole ordeal. She rented a room.

Bananas didn't only target customers. He managed to charm his way into the home of, not Gypper3—the manager of the station—but one of the owners.

Bananas and the owners were socializing together. When I came to work one day, I could tell by the tension in the air that something had happened. When I finally asked what it was, Gypper3 took me aside and said, "While Bananas was on duty yesterday he took all the money from the till and the safe, and then went to the owner's home and ripped off several thousand dollars worth of high-powered rifles, and a bunch of other shit, including more cash. The police are looking for him now."

The epithet *scumbag* is fitting for those of us that were in this line of business, but even more so for psychopaths like Bananas with no conscience at all. Gypper3 and the station owners were also scumbags, but the irony is that they were shocked by what Bananas had done. I've never been able to figure out why they were so appalled. To them, it was okay to hire a 50%er to steal *for* them, but it was unconscionable for a 50%er to steal *from* them.

~

My mom came to Vegas and bailed me out of jail for a weed-possession and brought her brother Cecil with her. He'd just been released from Tehatchapi prison after doing 21 straight years out of a life-without-parole sentence. He'd done a five-year stretch prior to that, so that made a total of 26 years in the joint prior to his release. Cecil was a classic *puer*—a boy in a man's body.

Because the police were at my apartment with a search warrant for whoever lived there before me, they were without search and seizure rights so the case was dismissed. By that time, I was familiar enough with the criminal justice system that I often didn't need the advice of attorneys, especially public defenders. A very important point that took me a long time to learn, is that attorneys (appointed or hired) are employed by whoever hires them. They can be fired if they don't perform their job satisfactorily. Fortunately, this one knew what to do.

My old friend Porker moved in with me again. I told him not to worry about employment for the time being, because I could get him a job working with me at Gypper3's station as a salaried gas pumper while he looked for work in the construction trade. Porker asked, "What if he won't hire me?"

"Then I'll quit."

"You sure seem sure of yourself."

"I am."

The next day, I called Gypper3, who was now the owner of the station. Later Porker and I met with him in the Nugget Casino restaurant in North Las Vegas. I introduced them, but Gypper3 was more interested in my coming back to work for him than acknowledging the presence of my longhaired hippie-looking friend.

"John, I need you back right away."

"That's what I'm here for."

"Good, good. I still can't pay you a salary, you know."

"Yeah, I know, I'm not expecting a salary, but I am expecting you to pay Porker here a salary."

Gypper3 looked over at Porker like he was a disease, and then looked back at me like I was nuts and said, "What the fuck for?"

"Pumping gas."

"I don't need a gas pumper, John, I have enough of them. I need a 50%er."

"Look, you have your 50%er," I said with a smile, "and I'm all yours, but you have to hire Porker on salary. We're a package deal and it's non-negotiable."

"John, you've got me by the balls." As Gypper3 arose to leave he said, "Okay, John, come to work in the morning and I promise we'll get him on by next week."

"No deal," I said as I started to get up and leave, "C'mon, let's go Porker."

"All right, all right, sit down. Goddammit John, you son of a bitch, you've got me by the balls. Okay, both of you show up tomorrow morning. I'll figure out a way to do it."

Porker had never worked in a gas station in his life, but Gypper3 laid off an experienced gas pumper and replaced him with an inexperienced one, and he let Porker know daily in attitude and behavior how he resented having to do that. Because of this, Porker did little things just to antagonize him, knowing that his job was secure as long as I was there.

I don't remember how long Porker worked with me, but it wasn't very long before he found a job in the construction trade and quit. Once Gypper3 was rid of Porker, the mere mention of his name would spark comments like, "Don't mention that worthless fuckin' deadbeat around me, he ain't worth a plug fuckin' nickel."

I was back and forth between Barstow and Las Vegas for a good reason during this time. Lynda, my ex, was living in Grandview, just down the street from my friend Jungle George. Whenever I was in town, I'd spend the night with her and visit with Snivels the next day for a while. If Lynda was with a man, she'd ask him to leave. Though we were not together anymore, I was still her main man and the father of our daughter, and we still loved each other. We just accepted the fact that we couldn't live together.

Before returning to Vegas, Jungle and I were sitting at his kitchen table with his wife. "Do you think I'm doing the right thing, Carol?"

"I don't know honey. That's for you to decide."

Jungle said, "I have relatives in Vegas so that's one good thing."

It was a big move for him. He'd have to uproot his wife and kids from a community they'd been in for several years. They'd talked about moving to Missouri for some time, so before he left with me for Vegas, he looked back at Carol and his kids and said, "Look at it this way—we'll be that much closer to Missouri." So I moved Jungle George in with me and Porker. I told Jungle not to worry about a job right away, that he could work with me at Gypper3's station while he looked for a job as a front-end mechanic.

"Goddammit, John, you've got me by the fuckin' balls again. How many more times is this going to happen? I hope this joker isn't as retarded as that last fucking loser you brought in here."

Once Jungle and I convinced him of his skill as a front-end mechanic, Gypper3 wasn't nearly as resistant as he'd been to Porker. The thought or mention of Porker always put ole Gypper3 into a huff. I still insisted that he pay Jungle a salary for pumping gas.

I'm telling the following story to show just how demoralized an alcoholic can get. In 12-step programs, Jungle's condition is referred to as incomprehensible demoralization.

My unfurnished apartment was still unfurnished. Porker and I were sleeping on the floor and now Jungle George was sharing the carpet with us. The first night that Jungle was in Vegas, we all tied one on and passed out.

The next morning, Porker, in a loud and belligerent tone of voice, woke up asking, “What the fuck stinks? It smells like shit in here!”

I raised up, sniffed the air and made a face and said, “Don’t look at me.”

Jungle rolled over and said, “Well I didn’t do it.”

Porker was up early and turned on a light or opened a curtain, then looked at Jungle and said, “If it isn’t you, then why do you have shit in your eyebrow? And why is it on your pants and on the carpet all around you?”

Poor Jungle started looking around and came to the very incomprehensible conclusion that he was the guilty one. “Oh my God,” he said, appearing embarrassingly pitiful.

Jungle had gotten up during the night and shit in the bathtub. That wasn’t so bad, but when he tried to get up, he fell back into the bathtub. He apparently managed to get out of the bathtub, but on his way out of the bathroom, he brushed shit against the doorjamb, and then smeared it on every wall that his staggering body bumped in to.

While Jungle was contemplating his humiliation, Porker and I dressed and told him that we’d be back when the apartment was cleaned up. When we returned, we found that he went way beyond just cleaning up his mess. He cleaned the whole apartment. We never did get furniture for the apartment. We just used the place as a flophouse for a couple months, and when the rent was due, we moved out with each of us going in our separate directions.

CHAPTER TWELVE

Criminalized Addicts

Back in Barstow again, I moved in with Terry and Susie. That's when I was introduced to Citra Forte, a pharmaceutical bronchitis preparation containing hydrocodone hydrochloride—a very potent opiate. Terry discovered it in Viet Nam and in Barstow he manipulated a local doctor for it. Dr. Woodyard didn't seem to mind being manipulated, for he was an inveterate alcoholic/addict himself. He was also a psychiatrist, but practiced only as a family physician. He was old and had been in the medical profession forever, and I believe he possessed the power in the medical establishment to get away with about anything with impunity. That's my guess anyway.

Terry said, "Richard, call Woody on the phone and ask him to refill your prescription for eight ounces of Citra Forte."

"But I don't have a prescription to refill."

"Don't matter, just call him and say that."

Before I could voice my doubts, Terry assured me that getting away with this was something he'd been getting away with for some time. "Okay," I said. "All he can say is no."

After I explained who I was, Woody only asked one question: "What pharmacy do you go to?"

It was as easy as that. I wouldn't, however, be able to call Woody back for another refill until enough time went by to have legitimately consumed it by the directions on the bottle. Terry and Susie had already already picked up their refills. Later, we started seeing how far we could press Woody before he cut us off, and it amazes me to this day how often and for how long we stayed high through Woody's unethical medical practices.

Citra Forte was like sap, in that it put our heads in our chest and was considerably more potent than any of the exempts that I previously signed for in pharmacies. Terry and I thought that it must work differently on women, because Susie often went on cleaning sprees. It seemed to work like a stimulant for her, whereas for Terry and me, it was a downer. Susie was taking a course in modern dance at Barstow College at the time. She had a dance recital one night so Terry and I went to watch. Of course she took a dose of Citra Forte before she left. One of the side affects of opiates is an itchy nose, and addicts can get pretty creative at scratching their noses in ways that aren't obvious.

While watching Susie dance, Terry said, "Richard, watch how Susie brings her arm across the front of her face."

I started laughing and said, "Yeah, she's using that motion to scratch her nose." We also noticed that sometimes she'd have to go a little out of sync with the rest of the dancers to scratch her nose.

I left Terry and Susie's place and returned to Vegas to work 50% for awhile. When I returned to Barstow, I stayed with them again—this time in a different apartment. They had friends who lived down the street who owned a service station. Gypper4 hadn't been in business long, and he wasn't a gypper until I arrived. He didn't know anything about merchandising and 50%ers, but after I told him about the high-dollar potential of his station, he was ready to make money no matter how unscrupulous the means. I had the station to myself until I brought my friend Gimmy in to cash in on the opportunity, then he and I worked as a team.

In the tall tale department, Terry was as gifted as they come. For example, he'd be telling a story about something that happened when he and I were together. Before long his version was so blown out of proportion that it wasn't at all like what actually happened. He'd even call on me to back up his tale: "And then we came up on this ten-foot rattle snake, ain't that right, Richard?" I'd usually agree so he could finish the story, because by then his audience was thoroughly engrossed and entertained.

I moved out of Terry and Susie's place and moved in with Gypper4 and his wife down the street. He insisted since I was working for him. He was a party animal and wanted his friends around as much as possible. His wife was sweet and naive and didn't mind having me live with them as long as the arrangement made Gypper4 happy. At my request, Gypper4 also hired Jon, my old sap partner from the sixties. That was one wild and crazy party station.

One day when business was slow, Jon told me about all the banks he'd robbed over the previous year, explaining how easy it was. He tried to talk me into being an accomplice by saying, "I'll do the robbery, Richard. All you have to do is drive the getaway car."

"No fucking way, Jon!"

"Why not? You're not taking the chance, I am, and you'll get half the money."

"But if we get caught," I reasoned, "we'll both go to the federal joint, not just you."

"We won't get caught, and if we did, you'd only get probation."

"Forget it, Jon, I ain't doing it. This conversation is over," I said and walked away. I didn't mind paying my lifestyle dues with short city and county jail stretches periodically, but I had no intention of risking years in the federal joint for bank robbery. That risky business was out of my league. Besides, his operation wasn't very sophisticated. It came as no surprise when I later heard that he was in the federal joint for bank robbery.

One day my puerile Uncle Cecil was pulled over by a cop in his old Mercury. "Can I see your driver's license sir?" asked the cop.

"Yes sir," Cecil jovially replied as he fumbled through his wallet.

When the officer looked at the license, he laughed and asked, "Did you know your license has expired, sir?"

"Yeah, I keep forgetting to renew it officer," Cecil replied with a sheepish grin.

They both laughed and the cop said, "Now really, why are you showing me a license that expired in 1945?" After Cecil explained where he'd been and that he'd just been released, the cop let him go, telling him to be sure and get a license. He never did and was never caught.

One night Cecil and I were riding around and drinking in my Chevy station wagon. We pulled into a Circle K, and there sat my friend Wilder, whom I'd worked with at Gypper2's station in Victorville. He came over to my car, and we briefly discussed the nature of the universe. Then I invited him and his girlfriend to come along with us. Once they were in the back seat, I saw a good-looking blonde, pregnant, and drunk. I introduced Cecil, and then Wilder introduced Jackie, but she was so obliviously drunk that I doubted she even heard the introduction, so we started cruising the streets again. Wilder was leaning against the front seat talking to us, while Jackie remained in the back rocking out to the music on the radio. Wilder said, "Richard, I've been robbing 7-11 and Stop and Go Markets lately, and you'd be surprised how easy it is to get away with."

Here we go again. "You go ahead and rob all the markets you want, I'm really not interested."

""Hey," interjected Cecil, "don't cut the man off like that. He's just trying to share what's going on in his life."

"Yeah, Richard, I've been making a lot of money with practically no risk. I just thought you'd like to cash in on it with me."

"That's real nice of you," I said sarcastically, "but I'm not in the market for a job in the armed robbery business right now."

A little later, when we started running out of booze Cecil said, "Hey, pull into that Stop and Go Market over there and I'll go in and steal a bottle of wine."

I pulled in, and when Cecil got out, Wilder said, "I'll go with ya and watch your back."

A couple minutes later they came running out of the store. When they reentered the car, Cecil said, "Go Johnny! Hurry!"

Of course I knew what they'd done, so I took off down a dirt road behind the store. Jackie, however, was still in the back seat deliriously drunk and rocking out to the music.

"You mother fuckers!"

"Shut up, Johnny. It's done. The best thing we can do now is figure out what to do."

"Fuck you, Cecil! Don't tell me to shut up. Who in the fuck do you think you are?"

"What fucking difference does it make now? "

It was my intention to turn on another dirt road and go out behind my Uncle Orvil's place, which was just down the road, but before we arrived there, Cecil said, "Johnny, pull into Roy's, we'll go in there."

I should've stuck to my plan, but in the panic of the moment, I did as he suggested. It was a snap decision in the midst of chaos.

Roy was my mother's husband but they weren't living together. He was living in a trailer where Lynda and I lived for awhile, which was next door to my Uncle Orvil's place. We all went inside and invaded Roy's privacy. Cecil didn't like the straight-laced Roy who was married to his sister, so he took a morbid delight in taking a bunch of drunks in there. Shortly afterward there was a knock on the door.

It was the police, and after some questioning, one of the officers returned to the market and brought the cashier back with him. The cashier positively identified Wilder as the one who robbed her, and she positively identified Roy as the one who left with him. Roy, never having received as much as a traffic ticket in his entire life, was booked for armed robbery, and so were Jackie, Wilder, and me. Cecil thought this mistaken identity was the funniest thing he'd ever experienced.

It wasn't so funny the next day when Roy was released and Cecil was arrested. My mom got Cecil and me out and hired an attorney, Leroy Simmons to defend Cecil. Wilder was the one who simulated a weapon behind his coat, but because he'd never been in trouble, he was given probation. Cecil's criminal record is what actually caused him to get four more years in prison. Jackie's parents bailed her out, and I went with a court-appointed attorney because I knew the charge against me would be dismissed.

I tell this story for the following reason: I called Jackie and asked if she'd like to go to our arraignment together. She gave me her address, and I picked her up. Her drunken condition that night was noted on the police report and her case was dismissed. I, however, was bound over to superior court, and a date was set for a preliminary hearing. At that hearing a month or two later, a superior court judge also dismissed my case. On the way out of the courthouse I remember thinking: *Yeah, it was dismissed, but I still have an arrest on my record for robbery.*

On the day charges against Jackie was dropped, we got stoned together, and every day after that we hung out together. By the time my preliminary hearing came up, we were inseparable. By this time she was six months pregnant, and only then decided against having the baby. I ended up taking her to L.A. for the abortion, then bringing her back to her parents' house when it was over.

Lynda and Snivels were living in Lenwood. Besides being emotionally unstable, Lynda was drinking and using a lot during this time. She'd often pass out when she should've been watching our three-year-old daughter. Twice a deputy sheriff found Snivels walking down the main highway by herself. The second time, Lynda was warned that the child would be taken into custody if it happened again. It did. After Snivels was taken into custody, my mom found out about it and was fortunately able to get Snivels placed into her temporary custody. Had she not known about it, Snivels would have been remanded to juvenile hall for temporary placement in a foster home. My mom was appointed a social worker, and for the first time in Snivels' short life, she was in a stable environment.

CHAPTER THIRTEEN

Suicide and Marriage

"I'm having a little trouble breathing today, Goat. I wonder what Woody would give me for it?"

"Call him and find out?"

I called Woody's office and told him my symptoms, and he directed me to his office right away. After putting a stethoscope to my chest, Woody informed me that I was having an asthma attack.

"I suspected that."

He wrote me a prescription for Tedral – a phenobarbital-based medicine. After telling him to bill me at my mom's house, I left, and Goat and I went to a pharmacy. I told Goat that Tedral wouldn't get us high, but I took one to relieve my symptoms anyway. But when I then started to react to the medicine, the proverbial light bulb over my head went on.

"Goat," I said with a smile, "I'm gonna have to call Woody back."

"Why?"

"Because this shit has jacked me up, and I need something to calm me down."

I told Woody that the Tedral was making me a nervous wreck, that I needed something to calm me down.

After asking me what pharmacy I patronized he said, "Go back to the pharmacy and pick up another prescription." Twenty minutes later I picked up a scrip for Butisol—a mild, schedule III barbiturate. Goat was familiar with this downer, saying that they weren't very strong. After taking a couple of them anyway and not being satisfied, I called Woody back. I told him that the Butisol wasn't strong enough, could he call in something stronger?

As though exasperated, he then asked, "What is it you want?"

Reds (Seconal) and yellows (Nembutal) were good downers, and Woody prescribed them to people we knew, but since I was going through all this trouble, I figured I might as well get the best, so I asked for Tuinal, (known on the street as rainbows in the fifties), which is a combination of amobarbital and secobarbital. He said that I'd have to come to his office and pick up a written prescription for Tuinal because Tuinal was a schedule II drug that couldn't be called in.

If looks could kill, I would have been stricken as soon as Woody's secretary looked at me. After motioning me into his office, I walked up to his desk and sat down. "How many do you want?" he asked.

In Las Vegas it was impossible to get a scrip-doctor to write any more than 30 for a schedule II barbiturate, so I thought I'd push it with him and ask for sixty.

Woody said, "The more you get, the less it costs per pill. Why don't I just write it for a hundred. Then you won't be bothering me anymore."

"Okay." By the time those downers were gone, my friends and I didn't want any more downers for awhile—they always spelled trouble for as long as they were around. By the time the Tuinal was gone, I had been arrested seven times and it would be two years before I was done with all the court proceedings and jail time.

I found a furnished apartment in North Las Vegas and moved in, and before long, Jackie and I were living together. I landed a salaried job, rather than 50%, at Gypper5's station near downtown Las Vegas. Gypper5 was a pleasure to work for after the last two unscrupulous Gyppers.

Toward the end of September of '73, I received a call from my mom. I was glad to hear from her until I detected something in her voice. "What's wrong, mom?"

"Baby, I have bad news."

Before she could continue, I said "What?"

She hesitated momentarily and then said with a cracking voice, "Lynda is dead, honey."

"What! My daughter is dead?"

"No, no, baby—big Lynda."

Snivels was four years old. Today, she only has vague memories of her mother, and for many years my mom and I skirted around the cause of her death.

Years later when she was around 13-years-old, she broached the subject again. "How did my mom die, Dad?"

"She was very sick. I've told you that before."

"Dad, what kind of sick? You and Grandma keep saying that she was sick, but you never say what her sickness was."

Whether it was because I was drunk or because I believed that she was old enough to know or both, I just blurted it out: "Okay, little girl... she killed herself."

Without looking at her, I could feel her staring at me, and then she asked, "How did she do it?"

"She shot herself in the abdomen."

I don't remember this conversation because I was drunk; therefore, I'm writing this from Snivels' memory, because she remembers it clearly and it affected her considerably. After blurting it out like that, she couldn't get the picture of her mom's death out of her mind for a long time.

She came to me a few nights later and said she was considering suicide, so I took her to a clinical psychologist for counseling. I don't remember any of this either, I'm just repeating what she told me. Much of my life that I am reconstructing for this book has been with the help of friends and family, in addition to my police record and work history from social security

Snivels wasn't raised in a stable environment. It amazes me that she's turned out to be the best mother her kids could hope for, and the best wife her husband could wish for, and one of the best human beings I've ever known. I'm grateful to have the relationship I do with her today.

Again living a somewhat domestic life, Jackie and I made periodic trips back to Barstow to visit our families, both of which were glad to see us settle down together. Our being settled down was an illusion, however, because we still abused drugs and alcohol as much as ever.

My old friend Dirty Dick, who was strung out on heroin and on the lam, stayed with us for a while. Though he didn't stay long enough for Jackie and me to pick up a heroin habit, he did share some of it with us. It was then that we finally realized why heroin never agreed with me. Dirty Dick didn't have very much to spare one night, so he only gave us a wet cotton each. After injecting mine, I felt great and I was surprisingly not nauseated. "Hmm," pondered Dirty Dick, "no wonder it always makes you sick, Johnny. All this time you've been overdosing."

"Good fucking thing, man, otherwise I'd probably be just as strung out as you are right now."

Herby was using heroin again too, so we also fixed with him periodically. Fortunately, Herby didn't come around very often because he was too busy maintaining his own habit and trying to support a family. Before Dirty Dick left, however, I bought his '68 Plymouth Roadrunner—Snivels used to call it *the hot rod,* because it was sleek looking and the mufflers sounded cool and it was a little lower in the front, which gave it a low-rider look.

After a couple months with Jackie, Jungle George moved his family into the projects. His cousin worked for the Las Vegas Housing Authority, so he managed to get one for Jungle ahead of the people on the waiting list. It wasn't long before Jungle's cousin acquired a place for Goat too. Being married was one of the requirements to qualify, so Goat and Big Head's sister, Della, were married. Jackie and I was the bridesmaid and best man. Also attending the funeral (whoops, a Freudian slip), I mean the wedding, was Jungle George and his wife, Big Head and his wife, and Porker. I won't go into what a drunken affair that turned out to be.

~

When I was visiting my mom one day, her anal-retentive social worker showed up. Here is what she said: "The judge will not award custody to you, Mr. Smethers, if you are on probation, so you'll have to wait until you've been discharged." I was on probation for my last DUI on Tuinal. "Furthermore," she said while looking at me over rimless spectacles, "when the time comes for the custody hearing, you should be married, because Judge Campbell will not award custody to you unless you are."

As soon as I terminated probation, successfully, I might add, Jackie agreed to marry me. Neither one of us cared to be married for traditional reasons, but we agreed that if marriage were necessary for getting custody of Snivels, then it would be worth saying "I do."

Goat and Della were the best man and bride's maid at our wedding. Whereas Goat and Della were married in a wedding chapel, Jackie and I were married by the justice of the peace at the Las Vegas courthouse. I didn't dress up for anything. I was in my service station uniform at Goat and Della's wedding, and I wore a t-shirt and Levis for mine. Jackie, however, for some reason, wore a full-blown wedding gown. Today, when wondering how I could've been so insensitive to others, especially those whom I supposedly loved, I realize that the selfish, self-centered, egotistical ass hole that I was pretty much defines the character of a drug addict.

After being married, we qualified for a place in the projects, so Jungle's cousin worked his magic and acquired us one too. The rent was cheap, which enabled me to better support my appetite for drugs and alcohol.

CHAPTER FOURTEEN

Prescription for Addiction

My old friend Dennis who introduced Gimmy and me to hitting cars in junior high school was living in Vegas, and he started something I repeated for three or four years. Dennis and his brother Phil invited my wife and me to go to, San Felipe, Mexico, to hang around on the beach, drink pina coladas and go fishing. Sounded good, so Jackie, Herby, and I followed Dennis in the hot rod. Snivels was with her Grandma.

We fished for corbina, catching sometimes two at a time. The Mexican skipper of the small fishing boat baited our hooks—all we did is reel them in. It was the first time that I enjoyed fishing. Usually, as with fresh water fishing, it was too boring waiting for fish to bite.

Herby and I went to a pharmacy in town to try to get some sap. When I asked the pharmacist if he had Robitussin AC, he said no. Herby and I must have appeared disappointed, because the pharmacist placed a little two-ounce bottle of something else on the counter. Herby and I looked at each other, and then I asked the pharmacist, "Bueno como Robitussin?"

He smiled and said, "Better!"

Herby gave him the peace sign and said, "Dos."

As soon as we were away from the pharmacy, we each drank a bottle. It was thick and syrupy, so we kept it tipped up for a while to get it all out. We didn't mind because it didn't taste bad. We noted the name of it as Tussionex and tossed the bottles in a trash can. Thirty minutes later we were making statements like: "We should've expected to get ripped off in Mexico," I said.

"Yeah, they gotta make money some way," Herby quipped. We both agreed that the cough syrup tasted too good to be of any real potency.

About ten minutes later I said, "Herby, I think I'm starting to feel something."

"Oh yeah? I was thinking the same thing, but then fluffed it off as wishful thinking. Maybe we should go get another bottle."

When we returned to the pharmacy, Herby bought another bottle. I was starting to feel the Tussionex even more by then, so I didn't get another one. Herby drank his second bottle, and by the time we were back to our camp, I was more stoned than I would've been on sap. In another hour, Herby was so screwed up that he was delirious. For the rest of our stay in San Felipe, he and I stayed high on Tussionex. Jackie also tried it, but she wasn't as hard-core as we were. Once was enough for her. Phil was sick from it, and Dennis and his wife were content with pina coladas.

The next time Herby was at my house in Vegas, I called a pharmacy and asked if they sold Tussionex. The pharmacist replied, "Of course we do but it requires a prescription." That's all we needed to know. Tussionex was a bronchitis preparation that contained hydrocodone resin complex, rather than hydrocodone hydrochloride or hydrocodone bitartrate like Citra Forte. It had an eight to 12 hour action, and taking it was like being *wired* on an opiate, rather than the downer, head-in-the-chest affect of Citra Forte and sap.

By most anyone's standards, I would've been characterized as a drug addict; however, having been a lube bay bandit for several years, I don't believe I would've been characterized as criminally insane or even a confidence man. I had needs, legitimate and illegitimate, and chemical dependence predisposed me to personifying the trickster archetype by which to support those needs. Having run the gamut of drug abuse during my life, my story of *physical* addiction is unique, in that I wasn't physically addicted to street drugs. I was a pharmaceutical addict for many years without having physicians writing prescriptions because I was writing them myself. In that phase of my life, it was difficult to separate whether I was personifying primarily the *puer* archetype with addiction potentialities or the trickster archetype. Certainly both in varying degrees.

When I entered Eastgate Pharmacy, I remember hearing that nauseating elevator music as I waited for the bald-headed pharmacist with the twitching, pencil-thin mustache to approach me. After handing him a prescription, he examined it through rimless spectacles and suspicious eyes, then looked into my eyes and said, “Be about ten minutes, sir.”

With an impatient but controlled anticipation for drugs and a feigned cough, I replied, “Okay, I'll just poke around in here until it's ready.” At that point my heart was pounding, but I remained composed as I casually looked over the array of vitamins displayed on a nearby shelf. At the same time, I kept a watchful eye on the pharmacist. He couldn’t see me as I moved over to the sunglasses rack but I could see him. Then to my consternation, he picked up the telephone, and I muttered to myself, *Fuck*! Feeling rage, despair, hopelessness and in dire need of a fix, I ambled out of the front entrance to the store; however, staying in the store risking that the pharmacist was *not* calling the doctor to verify the scrip was out of the question. Back in the car, I said, “Let's go, Herby, the bastard picked up the phone.”

The most common method of obtaining pharmaceuticals, even now, is to con doctors into prescribing them for supposed medical purposes, like I did in Barstow with Woody; however, there weren’t enough scrip doctors to accommodate a greedy appetite for drugs even in Vegas, and especially not in Barstow.

There were two other ways to obtain prescription drugs: by impersonating a physician over the phone or by presenting a written prescription. For the exception of the more potent schedule II drugs, many scrips could be called in over the phone. Each state is different. At the time California required a triplicate prescription form for schedule II drugs. In Nevada, however, a standard scrip would suffice for all drugs regardless of their scheduling. The scheduling of drugs is a rating system for their potency and their addictive qualities. Schedule I drugs such as heroin or cocaine are illicit, and cannot be prescribed. They are street drugs. Out of the pharmaceuticals, Schedule II are the most potent and the most abused, and then schedule III and so on, as I explained in chapter five. Schedule II drugs included narcotics (opiates) like Percodan and Dilaudid, most amphetamines and barbiturates. Keep in mind that everything I’m stating about the scheduling of drugs is correct for that time in Las Vegas. It may or may not be the same now.

Herby and I started getting pharmaceuticals by calling them in. When a pharmacist received a phone call from a physician for a controlled substance, the pharmacist asked the doctor for his DEA number (formerly BNDD number), address and phone number. When Herby and I started this scam, we didn't have any DEA numbers of local doctors; however, we discovered that all DEA numbers started with the letter A, followed by the first letter of the doctor's last name, followed by a six-digit number. With that information, we were able to call in scrips and give the pharmacist a bogus DEA number.

Being addicts, we didn't let being busted several times stop us, or even slow us down; being arrested just made us more conscientious. Before our many arrests, we didn't take enough precautionary measures to avoid getting caught, because we still needed to learn those lessons. For example, one day after Herby called in a scrip, we waited thirty minutes or so before I called the pharmacy posing as the customer (whose name we also fabricated), asking whether the scrip was ready. The pharmacist said yes, so I went to pick it up. That's when we found out why a precaution was necessary: the police were waiting for me.

I was booked for attempting to obtain a controlled substance by misrepresentation or fraud. Because I was in Nevada and busted on a charge that I didn't know anything about, I eventually copped to a misdemeanor and accepted one year of probation, no fine, and no jail time. During that year, however, I refused to go into pharmacies. Herby went in, or I'd ask Jackie to go in. If our friends wanted some, then they'd have to pay their dues by going in. Every time one of us was arrested, we learned from the experience, and started taking more precautionary measures until we'd fine-tuned our scam to near perfection.

Herby and I became proficient at calling in scrips, especially Herby because his voice was so official sounding, plus he'd heard a doctor call one in before. Here's the way it went: I went to a drugstore, found a phone booth close by, called Herby and told him to wait five minutes before he called in the scrip; in the meantime, I stationed myself in the pharmacy area where I could watch the pharmacist without him seeing me. I'd wait for him to answer the phone, on which Herby would be calling in the scrip:

Pharmacist: "Rexall Drugs, may I help you?"

Herby: "Hello, this is Dr. Goldstein. I have a prescription for you."

Pharmacist: "O.K. . . ." [pharmacist grabs his pad and pen] "go ahead doctor."

Herby: "For Floyd Gully—Tussionex suspension for eight ounces—one teaspoon every eight hours for cough—no refills."

Pharmacist: "Your DEA number doctor?"

Herby: "AG836572."

Pharmacist: "Address and phone number please?"

Herby: "763 N. Christy Lane, 453-1734."

Pharmacist: "Will that be all today?"

Herby: "Yes sir, that'll do it. Thank-you."

After observing this conversation, I watched what the pharmacist would do: If he picked up the phone and made a call, I assumed he was calling the doctor to verify the scrip; therefore, I'd return to the phone booth, call Herby and tell him that the pharmacist picked up the phone. This precaution is one we didn't take when I was arrested the first time.

Herby then directed me to another pharmacy where the process was repeated. When or if the next pharmacist started filling the scrip, I'd watch him for a while to make sure he wasn't going to call the doctor. I'd give him enough time to fill it, watch him a little longer, and then scan the place for undercover police while still keeping an eye on the pharmacist. It was important during this time that the pharmacist did not see me, which wasn't difficult because they were usually busy. Once I was convinced it was safe, I went over and asked for the scrip.

On one occasion when sitting in the parking lot, Herby reached into his pocket, withdrew a coin, flipped it and said, "Call it."

"Heads," I replied.

Herby grimaced, grabbed the written forgery, and went into the pharmacy while I waited. After several minutes, I started wondering if he was getting busted or just waiting for other prescriptions to be filled. What was going on in my head as I waited for Herby was frustrating: *Damn! I knew we shouldn't have come here. I bet he's getting busted. Shit, I'll have to call his wife again, and if she can't bail him out, I'll have to. Fuck! If the cops pull up and see me out here, I'll probably go to jail, too—then who's gonna get me out? My wife will leave and Snivels will be taken away, and then what'll I do? Shit, I hate that fuckin' jail. I hate sitting out here too. I think I'd rather be scared in there than scared out here wondering if he's getting busted or not. Damn! I wish he'd hurry up.*

Finally, Herby came walking out of the drug store with a cocky smirk on his face and suddenly I felt high on Tussionex before we even opened the bottle.

After a while we implemented more precautions and devised other methods of operation to simplify and increase the drug flow. We also made doctor appointments trying to con the physicians into writing us scrips for Tussionex or other opiates, but we also made doctor appointments for obtaining additional scrips for unwanted drugs like antibiotics, antihistamines and other non-narcotic medications. If we didn't get Tussionex, or whatever we were after, doctors always wrote scrips for what *they* thought we should have. The reason we saved the unwanted scrips was so we'd have *real* DEA numbers, doctor signatures, and samples of written prescriptions that we could learn from in the event we were able to rip off blank scrip pads while at doctors' appointments.

Every year I stole a new *Physician's Desk Reference* (PDR) from a bookstore in the mall, and I became very knowledgeable of its content about prescription drugs. Friends often referred to me as the walking PDR.

Tussionex offered the best high among all the pharmaceuticals available to us. We didn't consider schedule II drugs like morphine, Demerol and Dilaudid available to us, because of their high potential for abuse. Pharmacists were more apt to get suspicious of potent drugs like those. Herby and I agreed, however, that Tussionex was a better high than Dilaudid or Demerol anyway. The formula for Tussionex has since been changed. It now contains hydrocodone polistirex, rather than hydrocodone resin complex. It no longer provides the euphoric longevity of its predecessor.

One summer day I was in my yard listening to the buzz of the cicadas, when an old van pulled up. I watched the tall, pot-bellied, ruddy-faced man get out, and soon realized that he was my old buddy Terry, the one who turned me on to Citra Forte. He was living in Arizona at the time and was no longer married to Suzy. We greeted each other with a hug and I invited him in. After a few minutes of small talk he asked, "Hey Richard, do you know where we might get an Arizona scrip filled?"

"Why?" I asked.

"Because I have a whole pad of blank scrips," Terry replied with a pompous grin as he waved them at me.

"Oh yeah?" I said excitedly, "let me see that scrip pad," and then I wrote: Tussionex suspension—8 ounces—Sig: 1 (symbol for teaspoon) q 4 hrs for cough.

"What's Tussionex?" Terry asked.

"It's like Citra Forte but better and longer acting."

That was the beginning of our trial-and-error process of filling written scrips.

Not until we almost used up the scrip pad of Arizona scrips did we notice how poor the quality of the printing was. This set us to thinking. We figured if out-of-state scrips with such poor quality printing were this easy to fill, then surely we could come up with something equally passable, so we drew up a format that we took to a Quik-Printing shop. There was nothing on this format that suggested it was to be a doctor's prescription pad. There was no physician name at the top, and the DEA number on the bottom could have meant anything to a printer.

We went to a business supply store and purchased a rubber stamp kit. At the top of the form, we stamped in a physician's name and address. We used these scrips successfully for quite some time, periodically changing the stamp to a different doctor's name. Of course, this scam was before personal computers and the sophisticated scanners and printers of today.

Drug alerts put a damper on our scam. When pharmacists suspected a counterfeit scrip, they'd either call the police or alert another pharmacy, which in turn, alerted another pharmacy, and that pharmacy alerted yet another pharmacy, and so on until the entire city had been alerted. It was to the point where most pharmacists preferred handling the problem with just a phone call, rather than having to sacrifice valuable time in court as witnesses. Pharmacists making phone calls to other pharmacies, rather than a call to the police, obviously worked in our favor.

I took one of those counterfeit scrips into a drug store. The store manager (not of the pharmacy) recognized me from passing a counterfeit scrip in there previously. Evidently, *after* the pharmacist filled my scrip, he called the doctor. Of course, he found that there was no such doctor in Vegas. I was probably in the drug store shortly afterward shopping for something legitimate. When the pharmacist spotted me, he probably called the store manager and identified me. There was nothing that could be done then because I wasn't there to pass a scrip. However, a week or two after that I entered the store again. The manager saw me go to the pharmacy with a scrip in my hand, so he called the police. When I walked out of the store with a prescription bag in my hand, the police were waiting for me and I was arrested and booked for 'forged prescription.'

Again I used a public defender and fortunately he was sharp. I wore long hair and a full beard at the time. When my attorney and I were discussing my case, I mentioned my two friends who also wore full beards. His eyes lit up and he said, "Oh yeah?"

Curiously, I replied, "Yeah, why?"

"Do they have long hair too?"

Still not understanding what he was driving at, I said, "Yeah."

"What color hair do they have?"

"Brown."

"Then all three of you are white, with long brown hair and full beards. Is that right?"

My eyes lit up, and I smiled and said "Yeah!"

When Herby, Goat and I showed up in court, we sat together at the rear of the courtroom. When the pharmacist was on the witness stand, my attorney asked if he could identify the man who passed him the scrip.

He said, "Yes."

"Is he in the courtroom, sir?"

"Yes."

"Can you point him out for me, please?"

"Yes, he's one of those men sitting in the back of the courtroom," he replied as he pointed to us.

"Which one?"

"Well... I don't know, they look very similar."

"Then you cannot positively identify the man you filled—not one, but *two* prescriptions for?"

"No, I'm sorry, I can't be sure."

"Case dismissed!"

When I was visiting a friend in North Las Vegas, he introduced me to a man who could have passed for someone from an old 1940's Peter Lorre movie. He was about 35, skinny, short hair, with a short almost Hitler-type mustache, and with a face that looked like a mouse. I reserved judgment and made small talk with him and my friend. The strange little man reminded me of Igor from the

Frankenstein movies. Come to find out, Igor was a printer by trade. He was employed locally and had keys to the shop where he worked. After discussing the printing business for a while, I asked, "How would you like to have a free supply of some of the best pharmaceutical drugs on the market?"

A goofy smile crossed his face and he replied, "Well yeah, ha ha, who wouldn't?"

"Listen, I have a collection of prescriptions that I haven't filled. They're for antibiotics, antihistamines, and other non-narcotic preparations that I didn't want. Can you somehow make them blank again?"

"Yeah, no problem."

"Well, if you can do that, then we can make a deal right here and now."

Then my friend spoke up: "Hey, do I get some of the drugs too. I'm the one who introduced you guys."

"Sure, whenever you want some, let me know. and all you have to do is take one of the scrips into the pharmacy and get it filled."

"Fuck that! Sounds like an invitation to jail to me."

"Hey," said Igor while shaking his head, "I don't want to be going into pharmacies either."

"You don't have to. You're doing your part by making the scrips." All Igor wanted for his trouble was some of the drugs. By that time, we'd accumulated quite a variety of unfilled scrips: two from hospitals, two dentists, six doctors, and a couple specialists, for a total of twelve.

A couple nights later on Igor's day off, he and I went to Anytime Printing—his place of employment in the downtown area of Las Vegas, and there I watched him ply his trade. With the Eagles singing *Hotel California* on his shop's radio, Igor took a tiny brush, and with his nose wrinkling periodically, painted whiteout over the doctor's writing on the unfilled scrips. This process was very time consuming and required meticulous work because he needed to leave all the printed lines in tact where the doctor's writing overlapped. He took pictures of the blank scrips, then transferred them to metal plates, fed the plates into a printing press, applied ink, and started printing. An hour later we had thousands of blank scrips.

No more stamps, no more bogus DEA numbers, and no more calling them in. We had enough scrips to last the rest of our lives. With the experience we gained through trial and error, we figured we could continue filling scrips for several more years with little risk… or so w*e thought*, but there were still more arrests to come.

CHAPTER FIFTEEN

Squeaky Reincarnated

When my mom called informing me that it was time for my custody hearing, Jackie and I showed up in Barstow the day before our court appearance. "Mom, what if Judge Campbell won't award me custody?'

"He's the one that handled my case when I contested your dad's will. I don't think you have anything to worry about."

"Maybe you don't, but I do. Me and the courts don't have a very good relationship."

My mom was right. There wasn't much to it, and it certainly wasn't the ordeal that the anal-retentive social worked predicted. In fact, the judge didn't even ask if I was married. After the opposition tried its best to denigrate my character, Judge Campbell said, "John, you have nothing to worry about... you have your daughter." There were a few more formalities and then I pranced out of there as though Jackie and I had just given birth to my six-year-old daughter. After returning to Barstow, we gathered all of Snivels's belongings and took her home with us. I was happier than a mosquito in a blood bank. I had a nice nuclear family, my own business, and I was even on a softball team.

Dennis, with whom we went to San Felipe, and his brother Phil were on a softball team in Vegas. Practicing with the team a couple times a week, I was at first an outfielder, but later I was moved to the catcher's position. I think the reason they made me catcher, was so I wouldn't be drinking wine during practice. When I was in the outfield, I kept my bottle with me and took drinks out of it periodically. One of the team members gave me another nickname.

"Hey Port, play center field today," or "good catch, Port."

Around that time I received a phone call from Porker: "Little Richard, can you believe it? Me and Jungle George and Jody have been laid off again."

"Well, that's the construction trade for ya. Good money for awhile and then unemployment checks."

"Yeah, I know. Hey, didn't you buy all the equipment for starting a window washing business a couple years ago?"

"I did, and it's been in a closet ever since."

"Well, let's get it out and put it to work."

"I suppose now is as good a time as any. I'm working 50% for Gypper6, so I can come and go as I please at the station," I explained.

"Well, let's start early—how about eight o'clock in the morning?"

"Damn Porker, are you hungry or what? Can't you wait a couple days?"

"Fuck no. It'll always be a couple days with you. I know how you are. C'mon, is there really any reason we can't get started in the morning?"

"Wow, talk about high pressure."

"Look here, DeAnna is on my back, and my kid is screaming like he's being tortured. I need to get the fuck outta here, man, so do me a fucking favor will you?"

"Okay, okay, I guess we can start around ten o'clock in the morning and work till around two. Then I'll finish off the day in the station."

Gypper6 was a clean-cut looking guy but his appearance and Mormon background were deceiving, and they certainly didn't get in the way of his greed for money.

Herby sold me his old '62 Nova station wagon for close to nothing because he thought it wouldn't last much longer. He continually had to put water in the radiator, plus it wasn't much to look at. After I put stop leak in the radiator, it was fine, and I ended up driving it for several years. Porker and I loaded up the back end of the Nova, which we dubbed *the company car*, with window cleaning equipment, and at eight o'clock the next morning (not 10) we started teaching ourselves a new trade. I told Porker, "You da bwush man, Porka, you can't use da squeegee cause you too stupid."

"That's okay, Squeak, you da boss," he replied, and that's how we started Squeaky's Window Cleaning Service.

At our first stop I said, "Hewwo, is da managa here?"

"I'm the manager. What can I do for you?"

"I gave him a big crooked Squeaky smile and replied, "Hi dare, I'm Squeaky da window cweener, and me and my bwushman never weave stweaks or smudges and we come evwy week, and..." and I carried on like that, probably long after the shopkeeper was sold. Sometimes Porker would turn away or act like he was going somewhere because he couldn't contain his laughter. I didn't contain it, however, since I could imitate the original Squeaky so well, I found ways to cover it through my impersonation. I'm sure we acquired many customers by virtue of their fascination with such a strange character.

Here's an example, and Porker went along with this: when Porker was brushing a window, I'd pretend to get mad at him and jerk the brush out of his hand and start doing it myself, making remarks like, "Dammit, Porka, can't you do anytang wight. You a tewwible bwush man. I should fire you."

Then Porker meekly responded with something like "I'm sorry Squeak. I'll try to do better, but don't fire me, I need the money."

One of the times that Porker turned around and walked away was when I was pitching the owner of a produce shop who was currently stocking cucumbers: "I see ya windows aw dirty, da onwy way to get dem cweean is to hire Squeaky, da pwofessional window cweener. My custamas make wots more money when Squeaky does dare windows, and... "

The produce man stood there, staring, and listened patiently for awhile, but then he interrupted me by asking, "If you do my windows, what would I do when business is slow?"

"Oh, you can pway wit your cucumbas or smell your tomatoes or wash yo cawwots. You do vegtables, I do windows," and then I gave him one of those big crooked Squeaky smiles along with one of those goofy Squeaky laughs. The man shook his head, laughed and then said, "Okay Squeaky, you win. You can do the windows." I cleaned his windows for several years.

I grew tired of talking like Squeaky every day, so after about six months, I started putting less emphasis on my speech impediment and within a month or two I talked normally. What surprised me, however, is that not a single customer asked or commented on the change.

Porker's brother-in-law, Butch, was an ace mechanic and most of us took our cars to him. He eventually stopped working on our cars because he didn't have the heart to charge us for fixing them. Before he did, however, he agreed to fix something on *the company car*, so one day I dropped it off where he worked. He said I could pick it up at the end of his shift.

It didn't take Butch long to fix it. Business was slow that day, so he grabbed an old wisk broom and asked a coworker to hold it upright on top of the roof, while he drilled a screw through the roof from the inside into the handle of the little broom. When he was finished, it looked like the broom was balanced upright on the center of the roof. His fellow mechanic said, "Butch, what's this guy going to think about you drilling holes in his car?"

"Trust me, when he sees this car he won't mind a bit." Butch then took a plastic pale, like the one we used for cleaning windows, and bolted it to the roof, but this time at the back of the car, so it appeared like it was about to fall off. Then he bracketed a push broom onto the left front fender, and then a mop on the right rear quarterpanel. Butch and his coworkers were having fun customizing my car.

When I came to get my car, I was flabbergasted. Butch and his coworkers were sitting on a workbench waiting patiently for my reaction. I said, "Butch, this is a masterpiece—a work of art. You are a fucking genius!"

"Seeee!" Butch said to coworkers."

I have Porker to thank for helping me start a successful business that lasted 10 years. As expected, he went back into the construction trade and for the rest of his life he told stories of his life as a bwush man in *the company car* with the scatter-brained Squeaky as his boss. I had a whole succession of short-term brush men after Porker.

As a parts man at Ford and Lincoln-Mercury dealers, Herby was unparalleled. He'd been in the business since the early 60s. At this time, however, he'd acquired another high-dollar heroin habit. To finance his habit, he embezzled the dealership he worked at. When customers returned items for a refund, he made out the necessary paperwork and returned their money. Over a period of a few years, he falsified these types of documents and took the money for himself. He embezzled over $100,000.00 from his company.

He was caught and fired. It's hard to imagine, but several years later they hired him back again. During that hiatus, however, Herby needed an income, so he became my brush man. We were all over town doing windows, which made it convenient for us to run scrips as we worked. We had many accounts from shops that were close to the pharmacies we patronized.

The business didn't produce enough for him to survive, so I took Herby into Gypper6's station with me, and we worked as a team the way Gimmy and I did at Gipper4's. I did most of the selling, because Herby didn't have experience as a salesman, and he did most of the installations. Often he'd be installing while I was out selling. On busy days we did quite well.

One day I sold a woman a pair of shocks. Once the sale was complete and the shocks installed, she started backing out. Suddenly a team of officials from the Office of Consumer Affairs converged on us. The car was fully inspected before the woman had entered the station. Afterwards, the officers confiscated the old shocks and made another official inspection of the vehicle while she was still on the premises.

Herby and I consulted with a civil litigation attorney at the legal aide society, and he translated all the paperwork we were served with. We weren't booked into jail because it wasn't a criminal offense. Being a civil action, however, we were ordered not to resume employment in service stations until the case was resolved. The final disposition was a $50,000.00 fine for each of us, which the company did not pursue if we promised not to cheat people anymore. If we violated that agreement, we would be fined an additional fifty grand and both fines would be pursued.

"What kind of shit is that?' I asked Herby. "I don't care if they catch me again, I ain't payin' them nothin'." I went to work at another station as a 50%er for cash, so there were no records of my employment. There wasn't any record of our employment at Gypper6's station either—it was all cash at the end of the day.

My wife became attached to Snivels, but she wasn't happy with *me* anymore. She tried to talk to me about her feelings, but I either accused her of overreacting or just didn't take her complaints seriously.

One weekend, I went on a deer hunting trip with a bunch of guys and when I returned, my wife was gone. When I finally tracked her down I asked, "Why did you leave like that right out of the fucking blue?"

"It was *not* out of the blue, John. I have been telling you for a long time that

I'm not happy. I don't know how many times I've mentioned being lonely because you're gone so much. You're either working, chasing drugs, or out with your friends drinking."

"Hmmm, I don't recall you saying anything like that."

"Of course you don't. You always blew it off like I was on the rag or something. You wouldn't take me serious. Besides, how could you remember anything when you're loaded on drugs and drunk on wine every night?"

Because of my insatiable greed for drugs and alcohol, I became the poor broken hearted victim, and she became the dirty rotten bitch. I suffered with a broken heart for a while but my time was filled, because now I had to be mom *and* dad to my daughter. I washed clothes, cooked meals, paid bills, took her to and from school, did windows, worked in the station, and ran scrips. Sometimes Snivels and I spent time together in the evenings but it wasn't quality time—at least not for her, because I continued to drink my quart of Port wine every night. Fortunately I wouldn't pass out until after she was in bed.

Being a single father, I applied for Aid for Dependent Children, a fancy name for welfare, but government assistance still wasn't enough. I was used to Jackie bringing home a check every week when she worked at Frederick's of Hollywood. My dear mother was a top-notch enabler, however, and sent me money periodically as long as I didn't ask very often or for very much.

I was the one who eventually started divorce proceedings. There was a system in Nevada known as "divorce yourself." Anyone could go through this process without having to hire an attorney. I was with Lynda for three years and with Jackie for three years, which is typical for a *puer*, because they're continually in and out of relationships.

~

My little house in the projects became the place to go whenever friends from Barstow came to Vegas. After doing their thing in the casinos, they came to my house, or they came to my house and went back and forth to the casinos, or they just partied at my house and never made it to the casinos. It was *the* party house. The chaos Snivels was being raised around, especially after Jackie left, was not an environment conducive to responsible child rearing.

I bought a 1960 GMC pick-up, and then I bought a cab-over camper for it, in preparation for our next trip to San Felipe. When friends came from Barstow to visit, they often brought other friends with them. It wasn't uncommon for me to go to bed with one of them periodically. Whenever I did, however, I'd take her out to my camper, rather than take a chance that Snivels might walk into my bedroom.

That's how I came to be with Marcella. She was a party girl, loud and obnoxious when she was drinking, but lots of fun. During our first night in the camper, we agreed that she'd move in with me. I needed help with Snivels, and she had a little boy who was being looked after by her ex in-laws. The agreement provided my daughter with a mother figure, and Marci could bring her son into a familial environment with his mom. It isn't uncommon for addicts to enter into relationships on the spur of the moment.

Little Robert was an awesome kid and the new stepsiblings were compatible. I was not only relieved because I didn't have to do all the domestic chores anymore, but my daughter seemed to be happier when there was a mother figure in her life. Marci became my brush man; so for awhile we were spending 24/7 together, except when I'd let a friend move in with us. Then he'd take the brush and she'd stay home.

In October of '76 I was busted again, this time for another DUI and possession of dangerous drugs. When the booking officer told me to empty my pockets onto the counter, along with my keys came two sugar cubes of LSD, rolling like dice onto a gaming table. The officer looked at them, then looked at me and asked, "Hmm, sugar for your coffee?"

"It ain't mine!" I said emphatically while shaking my head.

Unable to contain himself, he said something like, "I didn't think it was," and then started laughing.

Marci bailed me out. I was sentenced to probation, a $150.00 fine and DUI school. When I walked into my first class, it looked like I might not have to attend any more of them. When I went home, I said to Marci, "Guess what?"

"What?"

"You get to go to DUI school."

"What do you mean, *I* get to go to DUI school?"

"Well, since you haven't been caught drunk driving, it's time you learned why you shouldn't be doing it."

Giving me an incredulous look, she asked, "Have you been smoking crack?"

"Okay, you're right, I'm joking about you needing the school, but check it out, Marci. The teacher takes roll by the sign-in sheet when you first walk in. All you have to do is sign my name and sit down."

"What do you mean, all *I* have to do?"

"Marci, think about it. Do you really think I'm capable of going to nine fucking weeks of DUI school without screwing up or getting busted for being drunk in class or whatever?"

"No, I doubt if you could do two weeks."

"Will you please do it for me then?"

"What if he's standing there watching when I walk in?"

"Then go to the rest room or something. If he's still there go somewhere else. If it looks like you're not gonna be able to do it, then come home and I'll go back and finish it. What do you say?"

"You better not get me in any trouble, Richard."

"It'll be a piece of cake, I'm sure of it. The whole time that people were coming in, he was at the front of the classroom shuffling papers and preparing for class. I really don't think there'll be a problem."

"Okay, but only because I love you."

"I love you too, and even more now that you're doing this for me."

The following week she showed up in class, signed my name, and not only completed the session but completed the entire course for me. I was happier than a nympho in a whorehouse.

By this time my window cleaning business was earning me an adequate living, and I often did a lot of bartering for services and merchandise. As I was cleaning the windows in a little shop that sold various types of artwork, pictures and frames, I saw a beautiful nude painting. It was tastefully done. It was art—not at all pornographic, even though it was a frontal breast view. This beautiful painting enchanted me. It still hangs in my study today. The shopkeeper let me barter my window cleaning services for the expensive frame that it was in, but because their paintings were there on consignment, I was required to pay cash.

Marci picked up a traffic citation a couple weeks before I bought the painting. When she went to court, she didn't have the money to pay the fine, so she was given a continuance. Later, she was given another continuance. When she received a third continuance, the judge was adamant: 'Pay it next time or go to jail, young lady." When the next court date arrived, I still didn't have the money for her fine. She insisted that I come to court with her and take the blame.

She said, "The judge won't accept anything I say, not now, so you have to come since you're the one that spent my fine money."

I did. I spent her last-chance fine money. Of course, prior to spending her fine money, drugs and alcohol took her fine money. When the judge called her name, she arose and walked up to the bench. He gave her a stern look and asked, "Will you be paying your fine today, young lady?"

Marci replied, "No, Your Honor, I can't," and then she turned around, stretched her arm out and pointed her finger directly at me. With emphasis and a quiver in her voice she said, "I can't pay my fine your honor because he spent my last-chance fine money on a picture of a naked woman!"

The courtroom broke out in laughter. As hard as he tried, the judge couldn't resist a snicker. After clearing his throat, he said, "No more excuses. This is your last chance," and we walked out of there one more time. This time I paid the fine.

The housing authority was in the process of tearing down all the old projects and building new ones for senior citizens. My house, among others in close proximity, was targeted next for demolition. My little family and I didn't want to move, but the housing authority gave us a deadline anyway. I learned through Jungle's cousin that I could force them to place me somewhere else. The housing authority resented me forcing them to place me. I was the only one who knew about and pushed that bylaw. The west side of Vegas was predominately Black. These projects were integrated, but Whites were the minority. I was convinced that they put us on the west side to punish us for forcing them to place us.

Not long after moving to the west side, my old friend Wilder, who stuck up the Stop-n-Go market with my uncle, showed up in Vegas and I let him move in with us. He became my brush man, and by doing so he also picked up a Tussionex habit. After awhile he wanted to detach and get a regular job instead of being so dependent on Tussionex and me. He found a job but he didn't have a car to get to work and back, so until he could get on his feet, I loaned him the Oldsmobile station wagon I'd recently bought. I'm not sure what his reasons were, but he took my car to work one day and never came back. I never saw him again. Fifteen years later, his brother told me that he died of some organic disease. *Poetic justice*, I thought.

CHAPTER SIXTEEN

Stability and Chaos

Encouraged by his half brother, in 1968, my dad made a will on his death bed. It took several years before the matter was settled, because my mom contested the will. Because I was such a misfit, my dad put a clause in his will stipulating that his brother, as administrator of the estate, would decide, starting five years after my dad's death, if I were competent enough to receive my inheritance. I was eligible to receive it in 1977, providing my uncle deemed me competent. Preferring to avoid my mother's wrath any longer, my uncle finally found me competent. Either that or he sincerely believed I'd become stable. "After all, he has a family and owns his own business in Las Vegas," he said.

For once in my life I made a competent decision. I used the inheritance to buy a new home in Las Vegas; we just needed to wait for it to be built. My credit wasn't good so the loan was in my mom's name. We moved into our new home in 1978. By the following year, I wasn't making ends meet, so my mom sent money periodically to help out. Again, though she didn't look at it that way, she enabled my dependence on drugs and alcohol by thinking she was helping me.

Perhaps my being an only child had a lot to do with my mom's enabling. The best way to explain why parents such as mine enable their children to destroy themselves rests primarily in their convictions. My dad and mom were old, having been born in 1900 and 1915 respectively. They believed that 'taking care of their own' was a parental obligation, no matter what road 'their own' took, and this is still a prevailing conviction among many parents. The extent to which this is true is clear in a conversation I had with one of my friends.

"Karen, I'm sorry to hear that your son is set on such a self-destructive path with his drug use, but don't you realize that giving him money and buying him cars and giving him a place to live is enabling him to continue what he's doing?"

"Yes, as a marriage and family therapist, I know that very well, but I can't help it. The therapist in me says 'tell him no,' but the mother in me is incapable of following through."

In many cases a mother's love knows no bounds. When my mom died, my aunt said, "Johnny, your mother idolized you. To her, the sun rose and set on you. There was nothing or nobody more important to her than you." My mom continued enabling me even after her death. The inheritance she left, provided me with enough money to finance two graduate degrees and the ability to live comfortably for a long time. She went to her grave providing for the little boy she idolized. Today, I idolize her for giving me such unconditional love. She never lost faith in me. She loved me as much when I was drinking and using drugs as she did when I was a kid, or after I became clean and sober and graduated from college with a bachelor's degree.

I have since asked myself: Would I do the same thing if Snivels started drinking and using drugs again? I don't think so. I believe I'd do what is supposedly the right thing to do and turn her away so she could hit a bottom, but could I really go through with it? I really don't know. This dilemma is one that thousands of people face. In my opinion, if parents don't enable their children, then the parents often feel the pangs of guilt so much that their happiness is compromised. It's a catch 22.

Today my daughter and I have a relationship I wouldn't trade for anything. It is worth my years of addiction, and even worth the years raising her when she was literally ashamed of me. Drugs and alcohol took top priority, even over her life. It is often stated that getting clean and sober isn't likely to happen if doing so is for someone else. I disagree. I would not have stopped drinking and using drugs if not for my mother and daughter. They were my incentive for stopping. They became my top priority. After I was out of prison for a while, I saw the joy and contentment that my new life gave them, then I had the incentive to *stay* that way. There is a big difference between *getting* clean and sober and *staying* that way.

~

A little over a year after my last scrip beef, Herby and I were arrested on another scrip beef. Goat picked us up at the jail when we were released on bail. The three of us were standing outside the courthouse talking: "Where do you think we can we get a scrip filled this time at night?" Herby asked.

"I think our best chance would be that 24-hour White Cross on the strip," I replied.

Incredulous at the conversation taking in front of him, Goat said, "I can't believe I'm hearing this. You guys haven't been out of jail five minutes and you're gonna do it again!" Goat wasn't strung out at the time, so he didn't understand our need.

Considering the circumstances surrounding this arrest, Herby and I decided we should hire an attorney instead of taking a chance with a public defender. A friend of Marci's hooked us up with her uncle. Harry Reid is a United States senator as of this writing, but in 1979 he was a practicing attorney in Vegas. We entered a plea of not guilty and a preliminary hearing date was set. Harry asked us if we were willing to take probation. I said absolutely not—I'd rather do time. The district attorney wanted us in jail for awhile, plus probation, and a fine. Harry tried to make a plea bargain, but the deputy district attorney prosecuting the case wouldn't budge, so a trial date was set.

When court date arrived and jury selection was over, Harry approached the DA again, hoping to get it resolved without a lengthy trial. The prosecuting attorney said she'd accept a $500 fine, probation and six months in jail. Harry told us what she said and our answer was no.

"Okay, it's your money, let's go to trial," he said.

At the trial, just about every time this young deputy DA opened her mouth, Harry would object and the judge sustained his objection. After about the seventh or eighth objection, she threw her arms in the air and said, "Your Honor, how am I to try this case if I can't talk?"

The judge asked, "Would you like to take a short recess?"

"Yes, please," she replied.

"Okay, we'll adjourn. Be back here in twenty minutes."

Harry approached her one more time. She said, "Okay, a three hundred-dollar fine and two years probation with no jail time."

"That's probably the best deal you guys are going to get, so I suggest you take it," said Harry.

I replied: "No, but you *can* tell her it's a done deal with a one hundred dollar fine and no probation."

"Now that's really pushing it," insisted Harry, "I suggest you take what she's offering."

Then Herby spoke up: "Maybe we should take it, Johnny."

"We agreed that you'd let me handle this."

"Yeah, but don't you think you're pushing it?"

"Herby, she's beaten. She doesn't want to go back in court and deal with Harry's objections. To me that's glaringly obvious." Then I turned to Harry and said, "No, tell her one hundred dollars or we continue where we left off.

Harry was only gone for a few minutes. He didn't have to say anything as he walked toward us smiling. I looked at Herby and gloated.

We shook Harry's hand and thanked him for a job well done and left, and we didn't waste any time going to another pharmacy. I saw Harry in Vegas several years later when I was there visiting, and I asked if he remembered me. He looked at me for a moment or two, smiled and said, "Yes, how could I forget the famous cough syrup case."

We'd gotten others and ourselves arrested so many times that most of our friends were ambivalent about associating with us. Their dilemma was based on wanting to get high on Tussionex or possibly getting busted for running scrips. Other than Herby and me, we caused three other guys to be arrested.

It was getting more and more difficult to sustain our habits on Tussionex, so we started writing scrips for Percodan, a schedule II substance. Percodan was so widely prescribed for pain at the time—like Vicodin is now, that prescriptions for it didn't create the suspicion that we'd created with Tussionex. We burned out Tussionex. Once in a while, if we found a new pharmacist, we'd get our old favorite, but usually we were relegated to lesser highs. For quite a while we wrote scrips for other hydrocodone preparations such as Hycodan or Hycomine, but it didn't take long for the pharmacists to figure out what we were doing. Pharmacists started refusing to fill the scrips, either because of drug alerts, or because they knew or suspected they were bogus.

Away from the projects and making house payments was an upgrade in living conditions, which gave the illusion of stability, but not much had really changed.

I'm sure I was considered 'white trash' by my neighbors. Marci and I had a lawn for a while, but it wasn't long before I let it die, and *the company car* was undoubtedly a horrific eyesore to anybody lacking the appreciation of such a unique vehicle. By then, there was a big dent in the hood and no front bumper, in addition to the dents and scratches all over the dull and faded brown paint, not to mention the way that Butch had customized it. No doubt my neighbors looked at me and my friends as a bunch of longhaired, refractory, and hedonistic scumbags. Compared to 'normal people', I suppose we were.

Not long after my dog, Bandit, came into my life, I took in another cute little white dog. For obvious reasons I named him Shit-Ass. Snivels was in a quandary about what to call her, because she couldn't bring herself to call the cute little puppy Shit-Ass, so to rebel against me, she named her Squeaky, after me. Shit-Ass wandered off one day and we couldn't find her, so I went to the dog pound. Yes, she was there. I claimed her, but they wouldn't allow me to take her until I agreed to pay for various shots and dog tags. Once all of that was taken care of and the lady was filling out the paper work, she asked, "What's the dog's name, sir?"

"Shit-Ass."

With a sigh and a bit of irritation she glared at me and replied, "I can't put that down. What's her real name?"

"Shit-Ass."

Getting more annoyed she said, "I can't write that down, sir! Don't you have another name?

"Nope. Shit-Ass is her name and it's the only name she has."

The reason I was being so obstinate was probably because the woman was the anal-retentive type—not unlike my mom's social worker, so I wanted to taunt her.

With another exaggerated sigh of frustration, she continued: "First of all, that's a cruel name to give a puppy, and you can't expect me to write down something as disgusting as that. Can't you give me some another name?"

"Nope, her name is Shit-Ass." I loved repeating the name and watching the self-righteous old biddy squirm. Knowing that she was about to blow a head gasket, I finally gave in. "I don't want to stand here arguing with you all day, lady, so just write down Squeaky."

With a sigh of relief, she said, "That's good, how do you spell... "

I cut her off and with a smiling face I said, "S-H-I . . ."

"Never mind," she said indignantly. She finished the paper work, handed my copy to me, turned around and walked away. Her problem with the ass-hole who named that cute little puppy Shit-Ass was finally resolved. It wasn't long before Shit-Ass took off again, but this time the dog pound didn't have her, or at least that's what they told me. More than likely, they didn't want to return that cute little puppy to a scumbag like me.

Once in a while, I'd get sick and tired of the chase and try to kick the Tussionex on my own. My attempt was like trying to fight a tornado with a hair dryer, so I'd usually give up after a couple days. The worst of the withdrawals happened when I was locked up. I wasn't able to sleep and spent whole nights tossing and turning in an effort to become comfortable. The cramps in my legs and arms were so acute that I couldn't hold them still. I sweated all over my body, even on my forearms and calves; my sweat stank like a foul-smelling poison coming out of me. I burned up with fever and then shook with chills. The symptoms are similar to the flu. I couldn't help thinking of that old junky that I was in the county jail with when I was 18 years old.

In 1981, when I was 36 years old, Herby and I enrolled into the methadone program that was run by the Southern Nevada Drug Abuse Council. After two months in that program, I learned that welfare would pay for my methadone habit if I transferred to the Clark County Addiction Treatment program. I remained on methadone for over three years because methadone is a legal substitute for heroin addiction; however, being addicted to any opiate qualifies the user for the methadone program. In my opinion, and in the opinion of many others who have used it, methadone maintenance is like jumping out of the frying pan into the fire. It's more addictive than any of the substances that people are addicted to that qualifies them for the program in the first place, including heroin.

After five years of domestic chaos, Marci left. She became involved with another man and moved in with him. Snivels and I missed little Robert as much as we missed her. I was mom *and* dad again, but this time my parenting skills were not adequate enough to contend with a 13-year-old girl who was embarrassed by her scumbag father. Not only that, but in her eyes I was old and didn't understand her generation. She once said to me, "Wake up Dad, this is the eighties."

I looked at her like she was retarded and replied, "Oh yeah, I didn't realize I'd been asleep for so long." I did my best but it wasn't good enough. Drugs and alcohol took top priority as usual, whereas my priority should have been Snivels.

I usually wrote cough syrup scrips for six ounces, taking one-once doses during the day. In the mornings I woke up about six and drank my last once from the previous day, and then went back to sleep until I started feeling it. Then I could get up and function without having to wait until I felt better.

One night Snivels had a nightmare so I let her sleep with me. I woke up early and took my dose of Hycodan, and then lit a cigarette. The next thing I knew Snivels was shaking me and yelling, "Dad! Dad! The bed is on fire!" We both sprang out of the smoldering bed. I told her to go open the back door, and when she opened it, one end of the mattress burst into flames. I managed to drag it outside and throw it into my back yard. Amazingly, neither of us was burnt.

All day I had recurring thoughts: *she and I both could be dead or seriously injured because of my fucking drug habit. Fuck me! The thought of her being on fire makes me sick to my stomach. I love her so much. What am I going to do? I can't go on like this.* By the next day my remorse was a thing of the past. I acquired another mattress and my life continued as though nothing happened. Snivels got in bed with her daddy out of fear caused by her nightmare, but her daddy caused a fear a lot worse than her nightmare.

Snivels used to beg me *not* to get a bottle of Port: "C'mon Dad, just tonight don't get any."

I wouldn't hear of it. "I worked all day, little girl, and this is my reward," I said. The truth was, I worked maybe four hours and spent the rest of the day chasing drugs. She hooked up with her first boyfriend during this time, but she was too embarrassed to bring him or her girlfriends around the house because Dad was always stoned or drunk and our house was always a shambles. Dad always seemed to have a weirdo friend living in the house too. I'm happy to report that none of them molested her, and for that I'm eternally grateful. The one that stayed the longest, however, was Artichoke Charlie. Snivels became attached to him. He loved kids, for he could relate to them on their level. Artichoke was a classic *puer*—a virtual party animal. He was a hard-core alcoholic, to the degree that my friends Jungle George and Hamburger were, but Artichoke also liked hard drugs. Hamburger and Jungle's drug of choice was primarily alcohol. Unfortunately, all three of them are dead now.

Although I was on methadone, I didn't stop writing scrips. I needed money, so I wrote scrips for greenie meanies (800 mg Placidyl). A few of my friends preferred downers to anything else, so I wrote scrips for them to sell. Placidyl was a schedule IV drug and relatively easy to fill. Why they didn't draw more suspicion, I don't know. For example, If I handed a scrip for Seconal (reds) to a pharmacist, it would be either an invitation to a jail cell or I'd spend hours before finding a pharmacist who'd fill it without verifying its legitimacy. Greenies were comparable to reds in potency. I also took them myself periodically; they were as much an invitation to trouble as barbiturates.

I asked my daughter to write something that expressed how she felt about her dad taking greenies. The following is what she wrote:

I hated the mood my Dad would be in when he was on 'greeny meanies,' so much that I took them from the cabinet one night and hid them in my room. I'm not sure why I hid them verses destroying them. I heard my Dad yelling and cussing at the man he believed took his dope. He threatened the man's life in some way and I felt afraid and guilty. I knew I had to tell my father that I had the pills. I was afraid of what might happen to me. Although he had never laid an abusive hand to me, I feared he might this time. With much courage I approached him and told him I had his pills in my room. He was shocked and confused at first. I explained how much I hated his behavior and how scary and mean he was when he took them. He seemed to understand and felt sorry for me. It was an important discussion and a life lesson for me. He talked to me very seriously for a long time. He was glad that I told the truth, but by doing that I could have cost that man his life. "Never ever take something that isn't yours, especially someone's drugs. It's very, very dangerous." He continued to lecture me on trust and honesty, not just between us but between him and his druggie friends, and the danger of that being compromised. Although he continued to abuse the pills, I tried to never come between him and his dope again.

With such a dramatic scenario involving my own daughter, one would think it would give me cause to stop using the greenies. It didn't.

Broke and under the influence of greenies, one night Herby and I decided to snatch a purse. Someone told me how easy it was at laundromats, so we went to one in Vegas. I told Herby to wait for me in the alley behind the building with the motor of my Chevy wagon running. I walked into the laundromat and sure enough there was a purse. I grabbed it and ran out the door as fast as I could toward the car, but something happened that we hadn't counted on. The lady's husband was in the laundromat and he came after me. In broken English he yelled, "I catch you! I catch you!" Just as I was approaching my car, Herby took off leaving me standing there with a purse in my hand and an irate husband coming after me.

Oh shit! I took off down the alley. Herby drove off in the opposite direction because that's where the street was. Running down the alley, I could still hear him, "I catch you! I catch you!" When I turned around, I noticed he was gaining on me, so rather than run any farther, I stopped, threw the purse at him, and took off running again. With him stopping to pick up the purse put a little distance between us, but then he started after me again yelling, "I still catch you, I still catch you!"

I was running out of breath and stamina, so rather than run any farther, I scaled a six-foot high wall, ran through someone's back yard, and crawled under a car in the driveway. My breathing was so hard I couldn't hear anything, so I didn't know if he made it over the wall or not. I heard my car's muffler, so I rolled out from under the car, looked around, and started running and yelling for Herby to stop. I finally saw the brake lights come on. When I asked why he drove off just as I was getting ready to get in the car, he said that he thought he saw me run past him. He probably saw my shadow or something else. Anyway, I was happy that I escaped my pursuer. I couldn't help thinking about Gimmy being sent to California Youth Authority for a year for doing the same thing. It would have been state prison for me. Herby and I needed money for drugs. Even though neither of us were experienced thieves, our needs drove us to it. It was probably a good thing we didn't get away with it because we might have continued doing it.

Snivels tells the story about how she and little Robert used to gauge what they asked for by what drug Marci and I were using. If we were taking greenies, they knew not to ask for anything. If we were using Tussionex, then they'd usually get most anything they wanted, within reason. If we were taking speed, we'd say yes, but tell them, "later." For nagging, of course, we'd get mad at them, so they'd have to want something pretty bad to approach us when we were on speed. Fortunately, for them, we didn't use speed very often. Asking for anything when I was drunk, depended on the mood I was in. If I were a happy drunk, they'd ask. If I was belligerent or cranky, they'd try their best to restrain themselves from asking, which is a difficult for kids to do.

~

After Susie broke up with Citra Forte-Terry, she hooked up with his brother Bobby, and they too moved to Las Vegas. When the younger of their two daughters was about a year or two old, they too broke up. Not long after that Bobby and a friend of his named Mike moved in for a while.

A couple weeks later, I started feeling bad—irritable, short tempered and physically uncomfortable. At first I couldn't figure out why. I thought perhaps it was the flu. I noticed that my weekend methadone takeouts tasted differently, but I figured the clinic changed the brand of orange drink they dissolved the methadone tabs in. When I returned to the clinic on Monday, the taste was back to normal and I started feeling better again. I forgot all about it until the following weekend. On Saturday morning I noticed the difference in the taste again. A couple hours later, I started feeling like I had the flu again. Then it hit me: *Fuck! I'm having withdrawals. Those dirty mother fuckers! They've been ripping off some of my methadone.*

I was furious. I grabbed my 22 rifle and walked into the living room. Pointing it straight at Bobby's head I said, "You take your fucking friend here and get the fuck out of here before I blow your fucking brains out."

Standing up very slow, Bobby started to ask, "What are you... "

I cut him off saying, "For stealing my methadone, you fucking scumbag. Now get the fuck out of here, Now!"

Neither one of them said another word. They ambled slowly toward the door. That pissed me off even more, so I shot two rounds above their heads and yelled,

"Go! Get the fuck outta here!" They bolted out the door and were far down the street before they stopped running.

On the previous two Fridays after getting my take-out doses from the clinic, it was either when I was busy doing something or asleep that they broke into my lock-box and took part of my dose, and then replaced it with a different kind of orange drink. They were the types of addicts who'd steal your dope and then help you look for it.

CHAPTER SEVENTEEN

Leaving Las Vegas

During one of the low periods of my life, Snivels and I were at home one night when the police knocked on my door. I told her to be quiet because I didn't want them to know I was there. Unfortunately, my door was unlocked and when they opened the door, there we were. Because it was another scrip charge, officers confiscated all the scrips that Igor printed, as well as the plates and all of my medical books. To keep my daughter from being taken to juvenile hall, they allowed me to call Herby to come over and watch her. When one of the officers took out his handcuffs and started toward me, I asked, "Would you please not put those on in front of my daughter. I'm not gonna try to escape or anything." The officer ignored me and put them on anyway. I knew that image would be indelibly etched in her memory for as long as she lived.

With her daddy continually in and out of jail and drinking himself into oblivion every night, Snivels was finally fed up. "Dad, I can't stand being around you drunk all the time."

"I'm not drunk *all* the time. Why are you exaggerating?"

"Excuse me, I forgot, you're not drunk when you're asleep."

"Very funny," I said, as if she were joking.

"Dad, you are drunk *all the time* that I'm around you. Why can't you be like other dads with a normal job and a normal car? Our house looks like Sanford and Son live here. This is a new house and it embarrasses me."

"Normal isn't all that it's cracked up to be, little girl. All families have some kind of dysfunction going on—they just don't let it show like I do."

Snivels shook her head in disgust and walked out of the room crying, packed her suitcase and went to Barstow to live with my mother. It was a courageous move for a 14-year-old girl to leave all her friends behind and start over.

Although I didn't want her to leave, I knew it was for the best because I'd learned that she'd been smoking pot. *Yes, it's best that she gets away from the negative influence of a bunch of budding drug addicts*. It didn't occur to me that it would be best for her to get away from the veteran drug addict she'd been living with for most of her life. Snivels didn't tell me until years later that Marci first turned her on to pot even before she started using it with her friends, so there was someone else I could blame instead of being accountable myself. Once in Barstow, however, she did what most children of addicts and alcoholics do—she started on her own drug and alcohol decline that would ultimately land her in treatment and then Alcoholics Anonymous.

After Snivels left, Artichoke Charlie moved in with me again, and we drank heavily doing just enough window cleaning to pay the utilities and plenty of booze in the house. Of course, I was still going to the methadone clinic every day.

One night after drinking in a bar, Artichoke and I started home. I evidently took my eyes off the road a little too long because I crashed into a brick wall. Someone saw the accident and called the paramedics. While I was being patched up, a paramedic said, "If I were you, I wouldn't be here when the police arrive."

Like most drunks in denial, I replied, "Why not?"

"Well, if I can tell you've been drinking, I'm sure a cop will too."

I couldn't deny this lolgic, so when he was finished with me, I told Artichoke that I was going to walk home to avoid another DUI.

I started walking on top of the block walls that separated back yards. Amazingly, I made it all the way to my house before I fell off the wall, right into my back yard where Artichoke found me when he made it home. I'd apparently knocked myself out from the fall. About a week later, I received a citation in the mail for leaving the scene of an accident and careless driving.

Snivels and I wrote letters and talked on the phone periodically. I wanted my daughter back so I kept insisting that she return to Vegas. She said, "Dad, the *only* way I'll come back is if you quit drinking."

"How about if I just cut down. You can't expect me to just up and quit."

"Yes I can. Quit drinking completely and I'll come back."

"Okay, I'll do it." After a little more discussion, we agreed that I'd go and get her. When I showed up at my mom's house, she wasn't home. My mom made a phone call and a few minutes later she walked in the door.

As soon as she saw the beer in my hand, she said, "Dad, we agreed that you'd quit drinking completely!" She then glared at me and started to leave again.

"Hey, it's only beer. Beer isn't really drinking."

"I'm not going anywhere unless you *stop* drinking alcohol completely, no matter what kind it is." Then she stormed out of the house.

I looked at my mom and said, "What the hell is wrong with her? It's not like I'm drunk."

"I don't know baby. I guess she thinks your drinking is a problem."

The minds of alcoholics don't work right. My attitude at the time concerning beer is common among alcoholics who drink hard liquor or strong wine. To me, and others like me, drinking beer was like not drinking at all. Port wine isn't champagne or even close to the more popular and milder types like Boones Farm. At that time a quart of Gallo Port cost ninety-nine cents and was 20% by volume in alcohol, comparable to Thunderbird, White Port, or Tokay, which were considered the rot-gut of the wines—the wino-wines.

I was appalled. I drove all the way to Barstow to get her, Snivels wouldn't go home with me. *That little brat, she just wants to stay here with my mom where she can do anything she wants.* Again I was incapable of being accountable for my drinking. My attitude was that I didn't have a problem with drinking and using, other people had a problem with my drinking and using.

Not long after that, I read a book entitled *Pathfinders* by Gail Sheehy. One of the major premises of the book was that making major life changes periodically is good for psychological balance and overcoming crises. The more I read the more I realized I was experiencing a life crisis. *Fuck, Lynda left, Jackie left, Marci left, and Snivels left. The only people who'll live with me are drug addicts and drunks. My window business is practically dead. I don't feel like doing a fucking thing. My nice new home looks like shit, and now my fucking car is wrecked. If anyone needs a major life change, it's me.* One of the major life changes the book discussed besides divorce, marriage, or a change of profession, was a geographical. That book convinced me, so I was going back to Barstow and move in with mom and Snivels where I could get my life back together.

Typical among the chemically dependent is the geographical. What they don't understand is that it's impossible to run away from yourself, for no matter where you go, there you are.

I informed the methadone clinic that I wanted to detox, so they gradually started lowering my dose. Against their recommendation, I asked them to detox me in 30 days. They said that wasn't long enough, it would take 90 days. I insisted. Although I didn't feel like I was still in withdrawals after 30 days, I did feel very lethargic, so I started writing scrips for Darvon N (a drug related to methadone) and Didrex (a schedule III amphetamine). At least I was then able to go out for a while every day and take care of the few customers that I had left.

In the summer of 1984 I found a renter for my house and returned to Barstow. Now my mom had two addicts living with her. The high desert was and still is saturated with methamphetamine. I dabbled in it before I left Vegas, but when I hit Barstow I started using it whenever I could. Detoxing from methadone left a void. With Snivels and me living under the same roof, we even used meth together once. With all my faults, I somehow didn't think it was right for us to get high together, and we never did it again. In fact, I used to lecture her on the evils of drug use. Undoubtedly, I was wired to the gills when I was offering such noble fatherly advice.

I started hanging out at a rowdy bar downtown called *California Country* and started hanging out with old friends who'd also returned to Barstow from Vegas, like Goat and Artichoke Charlie. Whenever Artichoke and I came into any money, we immediately spent it on speed.

With speed, we didn't have to cook it like heroin, and we didn't have to use binkies any more. Disposable syringes were in widespread use and relatively easy to get. Once tweakers start slamming, they seldom return to snorting it—the rush guarantees that. However, I understand that smoking it has become popular. The goal for me when slamming a quarter gram of speed (the average dose) was to make my brain feel like it was exploding, making bells ring in my head and make my heart rush with such pleasure that it made my hair feel like it was standing on end. That rush rocked me from head to toe. I loved the cold chemical taste that entered my nostrils and spread down the back of my throat as the speed hit my bloodstream. I never could understand why anyone would snort it when they could shoot it. I found, however, that Artichoke was an exception.

Watching Artichoke trying to fix was nerve-wracking. He couldn't hit a vein. He'd inject the needle, pull it part of the way out, and push it back in, pull it out again, then push it in again from a different angle. Again he'd pull it out and back in again. He did this in search of a vein, but he'd often get the needle in a vein and not be able to keep it in, so then the syringe filled with blood. Then he couldn't tell if he was in a vein or not. After all that, he'd pull it out of his arm and start over. Of course blood came out of his arm because sometimes he'd hit a vein and didn't know it. He'd go on like this for an interminable amount of time. There was blood everywhere and he'd have five or six holes in his arm for only one fix. After watching this a couple times, I said, "Damn Artichoke, gimmy that fucking rig. I swear, man, I wouldn't use a needle if I had to go through that." I decided that it would be a lot easier, on both of us, if I fixed him, so that's what I did whenever we fixed together.

Spending so much time at the Country as a customer, I started working on the owner to give me a job as a bartender. There was a band on weekends and a dance floor. After a month of nagging Gil for a job, it finally paid off when he hired me as a bouncer on band nights. Every time I hear the song "*Money for Nothing*" by Dire Straits, I can't help thinking of the good times I had in the Country. After a month or so, I was elevated to the position of bartender. Waldo, the head bartender, and I became friends and he taught me the ropes.

After I was sufficiently broken in and could work on my own, the owners put me in a little bar in the back corner of the dance area. Business was good, and putting me back there took some of the pressure off the main bar. I worked that little bar for a couple months during the remainder of the summer. Then they closed the back bar and I started working the main bar. I tended bar there, off and on, for over two years. I loved that job. Customers were continually buying me drinks and turning me on to speed, plus my sexlife rocked after hours. Those good times came at a price: two DUIs, another possession charge, and a public intoxication. After 25 years of using and abusing, I was still paying my dues.

CHAPTER EIGHTEEN

Freedom at Last

It's unlikely that I'll ever forget the third of December 1989. Snivels picked me up at the state prison in Jamestown, California in her Mitsubishi. This was her first car and the first time she'd ever driven a long distance alone. She was scared of breaking down, scared of being a young woman alone on the highway, and scared of the depravity of the lube bay bandits where she'd have to gas up, so this was a big deal for her but she was determined.

Our time together on that trip was more meaningful than any time we'd spent since she was a little girl. We went to Fisherman's Wharf in San Francisco where we bought matching sweatshirts. While in Frisco, we tried to visit Alcatraz, but it was closed. We drove to Reno where I told Squeaky stories, and then to Las Vegas to visit old friends. It was all good. We were higher than any drug could have made us. We talked about her mom, the projects, Jackie, Marci and little Robert, Las Vegas, Grandma, and everything before and after and in between. She was ecstatic that I was clean and sober. We were happy, and she had a brand new daddy, and because of her pride in me, I protected my clean and sober life like it was gold—for awhile anyway.

After returning to Barstow I continued the walking regimen I started in prison to lose weight. I'd walk three and a half miles to Lenwood and back again. Because I had no income, I talked my mom into buying me a bicycle that I still have today. Then I started riding 22 miles a day, which took off a few more pounds.

On those rides. I became interested in the desert's flora. I saw big beautiful white flowers that I wanted to know more about, so I bought *A Flower Watchers Guide* from the museum. I'd heard of the hallucinatory and poisonous effects of locoweed, but I didn't realize that the big beautiful white flower of Jimson weed was one and the same plant. On those rides I also discovered coyote gourds and the accompanying beauty of their flowers, which resembles a squash blossom. The plant doesn't produce gourds very often. The name "coyote gourd" came from the disdain that Native Americans felt for the coyote, believing that only a coyote is dumb enough to eat it. Coyotes are tricksters, but they aren't dumb. It's difficult to escape the conclusion that coyotes have a sense of humor too. How else to explain, for instance, the well-known propensity of experienced coyotes to dig up traps, turn them over, and urinate or defecate on them? I picture the coyote trotting away with that anthropomorphic smile that many people ascribe to their dogs.

My mom, of course, was also happy with the new me. I took her for rides in her car. We listened to country and western music together and watched movies, and I listened attentively to her reminiscing about her early life. However, the most rewarding aspect of the time I spent with her was the intense joy she displayed when we were together, a joy I never witnessed before I went to prison. If I were to start my recovery over again, being with her in the way I described, would be enough incentive for me to choose a clean and sober life. She had a brand new son, one similar to the one she raised. When I wasn't spending time with her or my daughter, I was attending AA meetings, three of them a day at first. I was still a junky, but this time an AA junky.

Because all the financial aid paperwork for Barstow College bad been completed and turned in while I was still in prison, all I had to do when I returned was enroll in classes. I started classes in the fall semester of 1990.

The first week of school was great. I was enrolled full time, taking 12 units. Before the first week was up, however, I added a computer course. I needed permission from a financial aide counselor to add one more class, which I did, and that was probably one of the smartest moves I made during my lower division work. Fortunately, I was already equipped with the typing skills for writing papers.

There wasn't a parole office in Barstow, so the PO made weekly visits and talked to all of the parolees in one day from that area. Because I touted AA principles and spoke in AA jargon, the PO was immediately impressed. Two months later when I was enrolled as a full time college student, he was even more impressed. I was placed on the honor roll at the end of the first semester. After that I didn't have to report to the PO anymore, and like Jerry and Lisa I was discharged from parole 13 months after my release.

I took to college life like a fish to water. I made the honor roll, the dean's list, or the president's list every semester and sustained a 3.5 GPA throughout my college career. During my second year at Barstow College, I joined the Alpha Gamma Sigma Honor Scholarship Society, of which I am still a permanent member. I must admit, however, that I might not have had the incentive to join AGS if not for a woman with whom I'd become smitten.

Several AA and NA members attended Barstow College, which is common for those in early recovery. Huck's wife, Debbie, and I took several classes together. A pretty blonde I knew from AA lived around the corner from me and picked me up for school every morning. On our first day, as we were walking from the parking lot toward our classroom, another pretty blond was walking a short distance away in the same direction. Mary knew her, so Mary1 introduced me to Mary2. When we took our seats in the classroom, there was a pretty blonde on each side of me.

The instructor was also a pretty blonde. Mrs. Heiden was the first Barstow College instructor I laid eyes on, and I was smitten again. All of those thoughts I was thinking at Jamestown to replace the recurring thoughts of my previous life, were happening. I found that I needed to shoo those thoughts away in order to concentrate on my studies. I was surrounded with feminine beauty, education, and the prospect of a new way of life—if I didn't weaken. I was on a pink cloud, but I was getting ready to fall off of it.

A couple months after I was cut loose from prison, my old friend Dirty Dick was released, so I gave him a call. That evening I went to his mom's house for a visit. We made small talk for a few minutes and then he went to the bathroom. After he was in there for five minutes, I knew what he was doing, so I tapped on the bathroom door. He said, "I'll be right out, Johnny."

I said, "Leave a little in the cotton for me."

"Are you sure?"

When I said yes he opened the door, finished preparing his dose, tied off and then fixed. After cleaning out the syringe and refilling it with what he left in the cotton, I took the rig and started to fix. Just when I was getting ready to fix, he handed me a belt, "Here, don't you want to tie off?

I said, "No, I don't need it," and I fixed in half the time it took him. I knew I wasn't going to start anything that would result in a heroin habit, because heroin was never my drug of choice. I didn't get sick that night either, but I still didn't believe it was a threat to remaining clean and sober. Getting high with him was a one-time thing and I didn't see any point in returning to AA and raising my hand as a newcomer, which is what we're supposed to do when we relapse. With Dirty Dick and me being the only ones who knew, my secret was safe.

I'd read and studied about relapse prevention in Project Change. I knew the danger signs, and I knew that associating with old playmates, playthings, and play places was a threat to remaining clean and sober; however, I justified the fix by telling myself that it wasn't a relapse. My definition of a relapse was drinking or using on a continual basis. I told myself that I'd remain abstinent after that one time. What I hadn't internalized, although I heard the phrase numerous times in meetings, is that our addiction is cunning, baffling, and powerful.

The next day I beat myself up pretty badly. *I am supposed to be working an honest program. I don't even like heroin that much. What's wrong with me?* The guilt really started eating at me during meetings, especially when they asked if there were any newcomers in their first 30 days. When I didn't raise my hand, I could swear that some of them were looking at me.

During my dump-scavenging days on meth, I accumulated three big trash cans full of copper wire and needed someone to help me burn the insulation off and then take me somewhere to sell it. Dirty Dick knew how to go about all that, and he owned a little pick-up to haul it in. A couple months after my supposedly one-time relapse, I offered him half the money if he'd help me burn and sell it. When he came to the house, he greeted my mom, and we made small talk in the living room for a few minutes. Then he excused himself to use the rest room. When he didn't come out right away, I walked over and tapped lightly on the door.

"Yeah," he said in a low voice so not to alarm my mom.

In a likewise voice I replied, "Save me a cotton." Then I returned to the living room, sat down and started chatting with my mom.

A minute or two later, I heard the door open and Dirty Dick said out loud, "Hey Johnny, c'mere for a minute."

I went in and he handed me a full syringe. I fixed, returned to the living room, and sat down. Because I was able to do it in less than 10 seconds, my mom was none the wiser. When Dirty Dick came out, I told my mom what I was going to do, and then we loaded up the copper and went behind Big Head's house and burned it. Because there were no recycling centers in Barstow then, we drove to Hesperia, 40 miles away, to sell it.

After selling the copper and splitting the money, he took a back way through the mountains to Berdoo so he could buy more heroin. I agreed to go with him rather than have him take me back to Barstow. On those curvy mountain roads he was making me uncomfortable. I said, "Dirty Dick, pull over up there on the right, okay?"

"Why?"

"Because I'm going to get out and hitchhike back to Barstow."

"Why, what's the matter?"

I said, "I'm scared. You're driving too fast and reckless."

"I'm sorry, Johnny, I promise I'll slow down. There's no need to get out."

Dirty Dick was in a hurry because he wanted more stuff. We made it to his connection's apartment and he went in. In a few minutes, he came back and asked if he could borrow ten bucks—he didn't have enough. I loaned the money to him, knowing full well I'd never see it again. After returning to Barstow, I decided not to have anymore to do with Dirty Dick. That was a hard decision to make, because we'd been friends for 30 years. I also proved the validity of the well-known 12-step precept of not going around old playmates, playthings, or play places. Again I started beating myself up: *Why am I doing this? My fucking life will go down the shitter again if I keep this shit up. I have to come to terms with this. What am I gonna do? This makes the second time. Well... there's only one thing to do: if I do it one more time, since a third time establishes a pattern, I will raise my hand in meetings as a fucking! newcomer, and I will continue to do so for 30 days.*

After going to three or four meetings a day for the first five or six years, I weened off to four or five meetings a week for the next four or five years. Meetings were a social outlet as well as a recovery program, and I enjoyed being there. It was an effort for me to share, however, and it wasn't long before I gave it up completely. Rather than give up the meetings because of my discomfort with sharing, I passed when it was my turn to talk. Sometimes I'd be asked to read, which I didn't mind. All 12-step meetings have members read excerpts from the literature, but first they introduce themselves, so before I started reading I'd say: "Hi, I'm a wino, junky, and a bunch of other shit, and my name is John."

It is strongly suggested to do several tasks in 12 step programs, and one of them is to get a sponsor. I met Rich at a meeting that was held every week at the marine base (MCLB) golf course. He was also the Education Services Officer (ESO) on base. I thought, *what better sponsor could I have than a counselor in education*? So I killed two birds with one stone. He became my AA sponsor, whom I rarely used in that capacity, and he was my guide through the education process. We're still friends today, and although we are the same age and have close to the same length of sobriety, I still use him as a mentor. One day in early recovery, I was at his house and we were talking about what it was like before recovery. After airing some of his dirty laundry from his nefarious past, he said, "And we all have stories that we want to keep to ourselves, and I'm sure you do, too."

"Of course I do," I said. "In fact, I have one that's pretty funny: Rogers is an old friend of mine from high school days. About a month before I went to the joint, he and I were in Newberry Springs visiting one of our tweaker friends. He suggested we check out the neighbor's house, which was about a quarter mile away. I'd never burglarized a house before, *but what the hell*, I thought, *I've been arrested for it enough*.

"Rich, I assumed Rogers was an experienced burglar," I continued, "because he'd been a heroin addict for several years. However, our combined skill amounted to what it would be like if Laurel and Hardy tried to burglarize a house. The front door was inside a porch that was open, and it was so hot in there that we were dripping with sweat, and we were still failing to get the house door open after an hour. We started arguing about who was the worst burglar when he finally grabbed the screwdriver and whatever else was in my hand, and said, 'Get out of the way, I'll show you how to do this.'

"I threw my arms in the air and walked off. I went around to the back door, opened it and walked in. When I unlocked the front door and opened it, Rogers looked up at me with a dorky look on his face and asked, 'How did you do that?'"

Rich and I both laughed and then I continued: "With a pompous grin I said, 'Face it, you bumbling idiot, I'm a better burglar than you.' I didn't tell him how I entered the house, but it wasn't long before he found out. He then complimented me on what a brilliant entry I made through an open door. We took a few items that we could carry and went back to our friend's house. When she asked where we'd been, we just said that we went for a walk."

Rich gave me some homework to do concerning the first two steps and then I left. The whole time I was talking to him, I was seething with self-hatred because I was living a lie. I shot heroin twice with Dirty Dick, but I couldn't bring myself to admit it to Rich or anyone else, so I detached from my self-loathing and directed my energies toward school.

I didn't want to lose momentum by taking a summer break, so I took two accelerated three-unit courses. By taking two courses in the summer, I was overdoing it. I took history and sociology. The B's I received for those courses would've been A's if I'd taken them in what was then a conventional 18-week semester.

In my sociology course that summer, I wrote a paper entitled Chemical Dependency that I earned an A on. I entered the paper in the *Desert Heritage Writing Contest*, and won an honorable mention in the college non-fiction category. After that I started gearing as many papers as possible toward addiction and recovery issues. By focusing on addiction/recovery for the rest of my education, I was building a knowledge base on addiction and recovery aside from my own experiences.

The part of the computer science course in my first semester that challenged me the most, was the spreadsheet program. It was during that phase of the course when Herby came to Barstow for a visit from Australia. As it turned out, I still hadn't learned that important 12-step precept of not going around old playmates, playthings, and play places, because Herby, Goat, and I spent the entire weekend slamming speed. That was the third time, so I honored the pact I made with myself. At meetings, from then on I raised my hand as a newcomer four or five times a week for 30 days.

When I returned to school on Monday, I was fine. F.I.N.E. is an acronym for **F**ucked up, **I**nsecure, **N**eurotic, and **E**motional. That acronym summed up the state of my mind pretty well, because I wasn't able to focus. Shooting speed all weekend left me *fine* and spaced out, which is why I wasn't able to absorb that part of my computer course, and that cost me the A I would've earned if I hadn't relapsed again.

Goat brought Gimmy's youngest son over to see me. I was doing something in the yard when they pulled up to the curb. I walked over to the passenger side, put out my hand and said, "Hey Pat, damn, you're getting old."

"Look who's talkin', old man."

"Well, I feel younger than you look."

"That's a good thing," Pat said with a smile. "Goat here tells me that you quit everything. Does that mean that you don't even drink?"

"Yeah, a drink would set me up for a drug. It has to be all or nothing. For me one is too many and a thousand isn't enough."

Pat looked at me incredulously, shook his head and said, "Damn, that is fucking amazing! My entire life is full of memories of all you guys being fucked up all the time. I can hardly believe it."

"It's really not that big of a thing. Anybody can do it."

Then the immutable Goat emphatically spoke up by saying, "But who in the fuck would want to?"

Pat and I laughed, and then he asked, 'Don't you miss getting high?"

"Not anymore, but I did for awhile. I missed the ritual of shooting up; I missed the dump where we spent hours tweaking; I really missed the speed whores; and I missed tending bar at The California Country. I pretty much missed everything about it. Then Herby came to visit from Australia, and he and I and that old man sitting next to ya, went out shooting zip for the weekend. Pat, I didn't enjoy that weekend at all. I was uncomfortable around the people we were around. I didn't like what we were doing, and I didn't like the way the speed made me feel. After I came down, I didn't miss it anymore—not a bit. More than anything, as far as the speed goes, I think I missed what I used to do on it more than missing the speed itself. Anyway, no, I don't miss it. The most important thing I can share with you today is that it hasn't been necessary for me to take a drink or put a needle in my arm since May 7th 1990 and I am real grateful for that."

I continued riding to school with Mary1, and it turned out that I had another course with both Marys. It wasn't long, however, before Mary2 and I were meeting in the library to study together. I was becoming more infatuated with her. She was married, but I justified my lust by saying I didn't know her husband. I was acquainted with the AA member whom Mary1 was living with, so I didn't consider her as a prospect.

The following semester Mary2 and I took a walking course together. On our long walks we became close. It wasn't long before she was picking me up for school in the mornings instead of the other Mary. Because she was married with two kids, I didn't hit on her. However, she was either very flirtatious, or she wanted something more than a study-buddy relationship. I was confused. She told me that she was happily married, but then at other times she'd complain about her husband being out of town so much. My experience with women for 30 years was inextricably entwined with drugs and alcohol. Now I was clean and sober and confronted with a married woman whom I *thought* I was falling in love with.

By the following school year we ended up in bed. However, I noticed that I didn't have a full erection during our first lovemaking session. I reached a climax, but I can't be sure how my impotence affected her. It was certainly reason for concern on my part. The next time we went to bed together, I was impotent. I was 46 years old, and this woman who was as beautiful as a Playboy centerfold, was only 29 years old. *What is going on here*? I wondered.

We did our thing through the summer of '91 before she ended it. During that summer, sometimes I was sexually functional, and at other times I wasn't. I believed, however, that I was morally against what I was doing with another man's wife, especially when we were in the bed that they slept in together. That would explain at least part of it. I told my AA friend, Yermo Larry, about my sexual dysfunction, and he showed me a passage in the Big Book of AA where it explains impotence as a phenomenon that's common with men in early recovery. Between my personal theory and the Big Book's proclamation, I was satisfied. From then on I didn't pursue any more romantic relationships. I was hell bent on education and didn't want any more interferences.

In both the spring and fall semesters of 1991, I took creative writing courses. My instructor for these courses, as well as for all the English courses I took, was a recovered alcoholic whom I first met in AA meetings before I enrolled in school. I'd written a novel and taken two writing courses in prison, but I wanted to improve my writing skills even more. I had hopes of getting my novel published, but I knew I'd have to improve my writing skills first. One of the requirements in the creative writing course was to submit an article to a magazine or journal for publication. I fulfilled this requirement tenfold before each course was over, and I also continued submitting articles (papers really) that I'd written during these courses, as well as papers I'd written for other courses. I wrote about my experience in Las Vegas with writing prescriptions, and *The Chief of Police* magazine published my article "Prescription for Addiction" in their March/April 1992 issue. The school newspaper also printed it. Later, it was republished in the 1992 journal for the *Desert Heritage Writing Contest*, in which I won second place in the college nonfiction category.

Having an article published gave me the incentive to continue submitting more articles and papers for publication. For example, I wrote about the *California Department of Corrections not* being a deterrent to crime. *Pleiades Magazine* published "Prison, the Day-Care Center,"in its 1995 issue.

While walking on the treadmill in my fitness course, I often thought about how incomprehensible being back in prison would be after being a law-abiding, clean and sober member of society for so long; however, in my dreams, I often do go back to prison periodically. I also go back to using drugs and alcohol. All addicts do. The dream world goes by its own rules, and the rules of consciousness do not apply. I have fleeting images of dreams past, but I am unable to recount an entire dream. As I write these words, I still have very realistic dreams of using and being in prison. I'm not sure why I still dream about prison, since I wasn't there that long. Waking up after these dreams makes me grateful that I'm clean and sober.

The Extended Opportunities, Programs, and Services (EOPS) office at Barstow College is where financial aide funds are managed. The office issues textbooks, hires peer counselors, enlists new college students from the community, and employs college work-study students. As a work study student, I first worked in the administration building under the registrar, then in the maintenance department, and finally in the library. After that I started tutoring.

If students earned an A in a course, they were eligible to tutor that course. If they earned a B they could tutor the course if their instructor from that course approved it. I tutored students in six or seven different subjects until I started working as a tutor in a computer lab. I worked in the lab for about five years, long after I was a fulltime student. I received a certificate in tutoring and an award for longevity in the tutoring program. I also used the tutoring program as a tutee, because I was, and still am, weak in math. One of my math tutors was Mary2, my married girlfriend. I didn't keep her as my tutor for very long because I couldn't concentrate on math. Mary2 was valedictorian of our graduating class. She had one of the most brilliant minds I've ever known. Being able to accumulate A's so effortlessly, no matter what the subject, made me envy her and want her all the more.

My mother was born on 12 June 1915. At 47 years old, I graduated from Barstow College, magna cum laude, on 12 June 1992. What a wonderful birthday present to my mom. I was also awarded a $200.00 scholarship by the Barstow College Faculty Association, and recognized as a contributing and permanent member of the AGS Honor Scholarship Society. The local chapter of AGS recognized me as a Volunteer Beyond Excellence and as a Wizard of Budgets for my two terms as treasurer. My mother and daughter were at my graduation, and so were many of my comrades from 12-step programs.

Chapman University's home campus is in Orange, California, but there were satellite sites called academic centers at various military bases around the country. In 1992 there was one at the marine base near Barstow. I started taking classes with Chapman before I graduated from Barstow College. About half way through the bachelor's degree program, Chapman pulled up stakes and left the base, leaving students hanging with unfinished degrees. Whereas some students forced Chapman to send instructors to do independent-study courses with them, I pursued course work at other Chapman sites around southern California.

It was Rich's job, as the education officer, to replace Chapman with another school that granted four-year degrees. He accomplished that particular mission with Park University, another school that's commonly found on military bases. I took my last five upper division courses with Park and transferred them and my Barstow College units to Chapman. In May of 1994 when I was 49 years old, my BA in psychology was conferred. I didn't attend my graduation ceremony at the home campus. Because I didn't do all of my course work with Chapman, the administration refused to recognize my degree with honors. My GPA was still

3.5. Chapman said I'd have to take more classes with them to be eligible for recognition as an honor student. However, Chapman granted me two $150.00 scholarships.

CHAPTER NINETEEN

Higher Education

After attending so many AA meetings, it was inevitable that someone would ask me to sponsor them. So when I was approached I asked Travis, "Why me? I've only read the Big Book once, and I don't agree with much of it. Rich is my sponsor, but I don't really use him for that. I don't share in meetings, I haven't worked the twelve steps, and I don't have a higher power. Why would you want someone like me to sponsor you?"

"Because I want what you have, John."

"What do I have? I live with my mother. I don't have money. I'm a full-time student, and I'm unemployed."

"I like your independence. You're not influenced by AA dogma. You work your own program and you're staying clean and sober."

What he said made sense, so I agreed, but my heart wasn't really in it. I hadn't worked the steps properly myself, so I didn't consider myself qualified to take Travis through them. So I gave him a Hazeldon workbook that would guide him, and he eventually did his fifth step with me. The fifth step states that "We admitted to God, to ourselves, and *to another human being* the exact nature of our wrongs." My mother was present when Travis told us all the supposed 'despicable acts' that he'd done. But the things he shared with us didn't sound all that despicable—at least not to me—so I didn't really believe he did an honest fifth step, so I kind of dropped him after that.

~

After two or three boyfriends, Snivels moved in with a man, and it wasn't long before she was pregnant. I didn't like the asshole at first, and I insisted that she get an abortion. She was adamant—she was having her baby. Against her educated father's wishes, she and Kenny had Kayla in 1994, and she became the center of my attention until my grandson, Jeren, was born in '99, and then they shared my affections. When Kayla was old enough to start talking, she tagged me with the name Gwakwa in her two-year-old attempt at saying grandpa. Today, I am still Gwakwa, which has been part of one of my email addresses since.

Fortunately, Kayla and Jeren will never see me the way that my daughter did. They'll never have to watch the police take me away in handcuffs like my daughter did. They'll never have to control their behavior according to what drug I am taking like my daughter did. They'll never have to endure being embarrassed in public like my daughter did, and they'll never have to write letters to me in jails and prison like my daughter did. With all of the light that had been surrounding me—my mom, daughter, and her family, there was still some darkness ahead.

One day when Kenny was at work, I went to the kids' house and said to Snivels, "I have some bad news."

Something in the way spoke caused her to stop what she was doing and sit down.

"What, Dad?"

"Grandma died this morning."

With a quivering lip and a breaking voice, she asked, "What happened?"

In an attempt to stifle my tears, I continued the best I could: "She fell down next to her bed... so I called the paramedics. They showed up within a few minutes, and as they were placing her on the gurney... I… I told her I'd come to the hospital shortly." I needed to take a deep breath periodically and use any method I could to keep from breaking down. "Because she'd been hospitalized a couple times before for low blood pressure, I figured she'd be okay once she was treated. A half -hour later, just as I was getting ready to go, the phone rang. It was the hospital, informing me that she didn't make it."

Snivels and I consoled each other for awhile, and then I went back home to the house that my mother had lived in since 1956. I spent the next half-hour crying. *Why didn't I go with her to the hospital and stay by her side?*

Once my initial shock was over, I realized that her death was actually pretty timely. When referring to Snivels and me, she'd say, "My kids don't smoke, don't drink, and don't use drugs." When she made comments like that, she glowed with pride. Moreover, she was able to spend a year watching her great granddaughter grow into toddlerhood, and she witnessed her granddaughter getting married to a man whom we both had come to love. She also saw her son graduate from college with a BA degree in psychology.

My mom was miserable for a long time. She still smoked and could hardly eat. She was so weak that I thought she might fall at any moment. In 1991 she let me pick out a new Buick, but by '93 it was necessary for me to stop her from driving it because she couldn't pass the written test for her license. Taking away her driving privilege was like cutting off one of her arms. She grew progressively more feeble, and often made statements like, "I wish the Lord would hurry up and take me," or "I wish I could leave this world." On 11 February of 1995 she left this world, and left me financially able to continue my education without having to get loans.

~

In my next creative writing course, I submitted a chapter from the novel I wrote when I was in prison. I must have sent it to twenty magazine publishers, and the most common reason it was rejected, was that too many authors were writing in that genre at the time. In January '96 "Cheating the Cheaters" was finally published in *Lost Worlds: Science Fiction and Fantasy Forum*. The novel, however, still resides on my computer.

For another assignment in creative writing, I wrote kind of an expose entitled "Prison—The Day Care Center" about how the prison system in California is not a deterrent to crime. Again, after multiple submissions, it was finally published in *Pleiades Magazine* in 1995.

In a subsequent creative writing course, the assignment was to write a romantic dialogue between two lovers. I was determined to write something different from what I was expecting from my fellow classmates, so I used humor to satisfy this assignment, developing not only dialogue, but the act of sexual intercourse between a woman and an alien from another planet. My classmates were quite amused, and I remember the instructor shaking his head and saying, "I wouldn't be surprised if some weirdo publisher accepts this." In Joon (that's the way it's written on the cover) of '96, the weirdo publisher of *The Atrocity* magazine published "Rangowl." Being published is an accomplishment usually granted only to those who are capable of accepting repeated rejections. Of course, there are those who are fortunate enough *not* to have to go through a succession of rejections, but I wasn't one of them. So it is with pardons.

There have been very few pardons granted in the Schwarzenegger administration when I last checked, and none in the preceding Wilson administration. Five years after convicted felons have been successfully discharged from parole, they can petition the superior court in their county for a certificate of rehabilitation. This Certificate is a court order, which declares that a person who has been convicted of a felony has been rehabilitated. If a petition for a certificate of rehabilitation is granted, it is forwarded to the Governor's office by the granting court and constitutes an application for a pardon. I was granted the certificate on 7 April 1995. Today, 20 February, 2010, I received a letter from the Governor's Office informing me that my pardon has been denied. I had to accept that as I did so many manuscript rejections. I can, however, reapply when a new governor is elected, but I'm not inclined. I'm 65 years old and don't feel it would do me any good since it takes 10 to 15 years for the governor's office to make their decision.

~

For years I had a passing interest in the American Civil War, but in my first history course at Barstow College I wrote a paper on the causes of the Civil War. I received a B, but more than that it sparked a deeper interest. After my mom died, I started buying books on the Civil War and its commanders and before long I was in possession of an impressive and continually growing library.

I took a Civil War vacation visiting battlefields and museums in the south, including the Gettysburg and Antietam battlefields in the north, as well as Fords

Theater in Washington, D.C. where President Lincoln was assassinated. I also visited my old buddy Jungle George, who was then living in Fort Scott, Kansas with his parents. All three of his daughters were visiting their mother in Kensett, Arkansas, so we drove there and joined them. On New Years Eve of 1995, after having a nice visit and a delicious meal at Jungle's youngest daughter's apartment, I asked Jungle if he'd like to go to Bourbon Street with me. I'd never been to New Orleans and wanted to see it.

On the way, we talked about the old days in Barstow and Las Vegas. It was New Years Eve in New Orleans, and we finally found a parking space and patronized some of the shops on Bourbon Street. It wasn't long before I started feeling squirrelly. The festivities were starting already and it wasn't even dark yet. I said, "Jungle, I'm getting uncomfortable here. I'm afraid if I stay here with all this partying goin' on, I'm gonna want to drink."

"If you've been sober for five years, I don't see a problem."

"It doesn't go away, Jungle."

"Well I'm gonna have a couple drinks."

When he said that I went off on him. I can't remember everything I said, but I was appalled that he'd jeopardize my recovery by drinking around me. After I ranted and raged for a while, he said, "Okay, okay! Fuck, I don't *have* to drink. Calm down."

We searched and searched and finally found a vacant motel room with two beds about 50 miles from New Orleans. By that time, I was tired, so I went to bed and thought Jungle did too. About five o'clock in the morning, I heard some shuffling around and Jungle mumbling to himself. I could tell by his voice that he'd been drinking. It was too late to pitch a bitch about it then, and he wasn't really all that drunk, but it still pissed me off, so I gave him the silent treatment for most of the way back. When we were approaching Kansas, I started softening some. Although we parted on good terms, I was still resentful.

The following year, I flew to Philadelphia, rented a car, and drove to Gettysburg for the annual re-enactment on July 1st, 2nd, and 3rd. The battle was a monstrous affair. I enjoyed watching all the cannons going off one after the other, the re-enactors loading, shooting, and reloading their muskets, and the tactical maneuvers. It was all serious business, recreating what actually happened. If I would've known what the re-enactment was going to actually be like, I would've been better prepared to enjoy it. As it was, I was overwhelmed by the magnitude of it all. What I did enjoy, however, was visiting where General Joshua Chamberlain led his famous bayonet charge down Little Round Top, and visiting the brick wall where Pickett's charge came to such a devastating end.

While I was in Gettysburg, I looked up my old friend Waldo, the man who trained me as a bartender. We had a nice visit talking about the crazy days in The California Country, and discussing all the people we drank and used with

After returning to Barstow, I started applying to graduate schools for a master's degree. During the next two years I applied to several schools. I was interviewed at two of them, and rejected by both. During that two-year period, I also continued my obsession with my growing Civil War library. Today it consists of over 500 books.

When alcoholics and addicts refrain from their addiction, it's not uncommon for them to transfer their obsessive/compulsive behavior from chemical substances to other addictions such as sex, food, gambling, and work. I was no different. I became addicted to education and the American Civil War.

While I was waiting for a third graduate school rejection, Rich (my supposed sponsor and counselor) negotiated a deal with National University in San Diego to offer a Master of Human Services (MHS) degree in Community Psychology at the base. The arrangement was that the first four courses would earn students a certificate in Community Psychology and Human Services. Then it was supposed to roll over into a master's degree program, with the four classes serving as core courses for the masters. However, National reneged after the first four courses, and like Chapman they pulled up stakes and left. I was the only student in the program who pursued the degree in San Diego.

When I realized I was going to commute to San Diego for classes, I bought a new truck and a cab-over camper. I drove to San Diego on Tuesday, attended class that night and slept in my camper. I stayed in the San Diego area and did research for school, visited used bookstores, and went to movies, until my next class on Thursday night. Then I returned home, and I traveled every week until I needed to start doing my Work Experience and Practicum course work.

During my course work I had an experience worth mentioning. The course was Relational Violence and the instructor required students to give a preapproved presentation in addition to a traditional research paper. I was one of the first students to present. The following week I turned in my paper. The week after that, the instructor called me up to her desk and asked, "John, did you have help writing this paper?"

I couldn't believe what she was asking me. I replied, "No. I've been writing my own papers for about eight years now."

"This paper is written very well, John, which is in contrast to how you speak. After listening to your presentation last week and then reading your paper, I found a profound contrast."

"It could be that I'm a good writer and not a very good speaker, ma'am."

"John, I'm not trying to insult you. I'm sure you can see how I'd come to this conclusion."

"If it's any consolation, ma'am, I've been published five times."

"Oh? Could I read one of them?"

On my way to my book-bag I thought, *what is she trying to pull? I bet she doesn't like to give As, so she's building a case so she doesn't have to.* I pulled all five of them out and spread them on the table before her.

"Oh," she said, like she was surprised "you have them with you?"

Good thing! I thought. When I speak, I still sound the way I did before recovery. I don't write the way I speak, so hopefully my venerable instructor learned a lesson.

By the time we finished talking, I wasn't offended anymore because she convinced me that her suspicions had merit. When she returned my magazine article the following week, she said, "John, you are a walking dichotomy. Again, let me apologize for misunderstanding you." She gave me a B anyway, probably because of my lack of speaking ability.

In my Field Experience course, I was an intern at the McAlister Institute in San Diego. In their outpatient detox program, I attended staff meetings and interviewed the operations director about administrative and managerial operations. I also attended outpatient detox groups where I helped facilitate a group in self-disclosure, one in anger management, another in medical aspects of recovery, and a group that introduced the 12 steps. Being in San Diego for only one day a week between classes, didn't give me enough time to accumulate enough work-experience hours before graduation, so I took my camper off and commuted for each class twice a week. San Diego is 190 miles from Barstow, so I spent a lot of time on the road.

I had friends who were volunteers for the Project Focus program sponsored by the San Bernardino County Probation Department in Barstow. One of them was a Marriage and Family Therapist (MFT) who ran the Freedom From Substance Abuse for Youth group. I worked with him in this family-centered group where we, as facilitators, worked with parents as well as their kids. After we conducted enrollments and drug and alcohol assessments, we did various exercises, brought in NA and AA panels to share experience, strength, and hope, and discussed matters such as impediments to success because of drugs and alcohol. The last session in which we discussed what the group learned over the previous 12 weeks, included parents. The session ended with certificates of completion, pizza and soda.

When I first met my co-facilitator in AA meetings, I respected him because of his education, but after working with him in the Project Focus program, I saw a side of him I hadn't seen before. He didn't treat the kids with respect, often making derogatory remarks to them and treating them like they were stupid. Maybe that was his style, or maybe it was an accepted approach like tough love, but I don't believe therapy done in that way can be successful very often. I think my co-facilitator contributed to the prophecy in the title of James Hillman's book *We've Had a Hundred Years of Psychotherapy and the World's Getting Worse.*

I wanted to get a medley of work experience so I chose a variety. I went to the marine base and was allowed to develop the Retired Affairs Office (RAO). One of the required courses I took for my masters was Program Development and Evaluation, so this was an opportunity to apply what I'd learned in the course and to get experience in the field. By the time I was finished with the RAO, the director of the Family Services Center was so impressed with my energy and performance that he was glad to have me on board when I applied for a job as a library technician a couple years later.

I did my Practicum in one place, at the marine base in the Career Resource Management Center. I assisted clients in developing resumes and assisted with intake interviews. A counselor and I developed a brief telephone survey to determine how the CRMC could be improved. Again, my course in program development and evaluation were helpful. I attended staff meetings and familiarized myself with the books and videos on public speaking, self-esteem, assertiveness training, job search services, social maturity, and professional phone skills. When I was finished with my 150-hour Practicum course, I was finished with all the requirements for my degree except the comprehensive examination, which I easily passed.

In April of 1998, my Master of Human Services in Community Psychology was conferred, and I was awarded the certificate as well. Again, I didn't attend my graduation ceremony. By that time I viewed my BA and MHS as stepping stones to the Ph.D. that I coveted.

CHAPTER TWENTY

Doctor of Philosophy

As a reward for earning my masters I went on another Civil War vacation, but this time I didn't go alone. There was one person who shared with me a genuine interest in the Civil War, my friend Crazy. He, however, was a practicing addict, but since I knew his Civil War interest was genuine, I asked him to go along anyway. At first, he was ambivalent. He wanted to go but, he knew I'd insist he stay clean. I gave him time to think about the trip, and when I approached him again, he decided to go with me.

"I'm curious about something though," asked Crazy.

"What?"

"Where are we going to take showers? You may have two beds and a kitchen, but you don't have a shower in that little camper."

"Yeah I do, but it's on the outside."

"You mean we have to stand outside in our birthday suits to take showers?"

"Yep, we'll find shower roads." And we did. We found some strange places to take showers. One of them was in back of a derelict gas station. When we were down South, we found shower roads that went off into the woods.

We loaded my truck and camper and left. Crazy did okay until we arrived at Michele's place in Los Cruces, New Mexico. We both drank and used with Michelle before she left Barstow. In Las Cruces she was active in NA, had a good job, and seemed happy. Crazy wasn't happy, however. The next morning, before I awoke, he talked Michelle into taking him to the Veteran's hospital to get treated for a headache. The attending physician checked him out and wrote him a prescription.

When they returned, I asked, "Where did you go?"

"Crazy asked me to take him to the hospital for his headache."

"So how's your headache, Crazy?"

"Whatever that fucking quack gave me, it isn't working."

"Of course it isn't," I said laughingly, "because it isn't something that'll get you high."

"Fuck you."

Unfortunately, that situation set up what is known as the phenomenon of craving, which put a strain on our trip and especially on our relationship. We hung out with Michelle for a couple more hours and then left.

We then stopped in San Antonio to see Crazy's mother. She was happy to see us, and we spent the night. The next morning before I awoke, Crazy told his mother about his headaches, and he persuaded her to call her doctor for an emergency visit.

I didn't get up until they returned. Crazy's mom fixed us breakfast and talked us into staying another night. That day Crazy and I went to the Alamo. We took pictures of each other and bought souvenirs and actually enjoyed ourselves, but something about Crazy was bothering me, so I needed to say something: "Crazy, I bet you don't have a headache now."

"No, as a matter of fact, I feel very good today," he replied amicably.

"What did you steal out of your mother's medicine cabinet?" I asked casually.

"Give me a fucking break. Do you really think I'd do that?"

"Yeah, I do."

"Do I have to be loaded to be in a good mood and enjoy myself?"

"Are you telling me you're not loaded?"

"Darvon, Richard. Darvon. How fucking loaded have you ever been on Darvon?"

He was right. The only thing Darvon ever did for me, was make my aching bones feel better when I was kicking Tussionex or Methadone.

Crazy spent some seemingly quality time with his mother, staying up late that night, going through photo albums, and talking about his brother and their childhoods. Before leaving the next morning, Crazy's mom gave him a couple hundred dollars to take some of the strain off me.

After leaving San Antonio, we visited some other sites in the state, including Barstow, Texas, before we left for Fort Smith, Arkansas to visit an AA member who once lived in Barstow. Crazy could decorate a Christmas tree with the many newcomer chips he'd received by then, and like me, he made lasting friendships. Terry was one of them. We went to a couple meetings with Terry and his wife, visited the local museums, and spent the night. Crazy's behavior puzzled me. He acted like he was on opiates, which was his preference over all others.

I talked him into letting me dole out the pills to him, so he wouldn't go through them so fast. Sometimes his supossed headaches were worse than usual, so I let him have more, rather than argue with him. I finally came to realize that Crazy actually liked Darvon. I'd never heard of that. Everyone I ever knew thought of Darvon as useless for getting high.

When we left Fort Smith, it wasn't far to the residence of an old friend of mine whom I'd originally met at Camp Snoopy in '65. Floyd lived in the backwoods of Arkansas, in some town, the name of which escapes me. We had a nice visit and Floyd's wife made a home video of us. The only problem with visiting Floyd was that he was also a practicing addict, and he generously turned on Crazy while we were there. Floyd's dependence on drugs, according to him, was the result of car accidents; therefore, he sustains a habit on strong painkillers prescribed by physicians. However, in the old days, he and I used drugs recreationally over a period of 25 years; therefore, I tend to be suspicious of anyone claiming dependence on pain killers for medical reasons, especially people I've used drugs with recreationally. The time Crazy and I spent with Floyd is probably the closest I came to using drugs since my last relapse with Goat and Herby in1990. Floyd wanted us to stay longer, but there was no way I could stay any longer and stay clean. I have since come to accept that Floyd's dependence on painkillers is a medical necessity. However, I'm not claiming that he doesn't enjoy the high, and I'd bet that he uses more than what's prescribed.

Our next stop was in Fort Scott, Kansas, to see Jungle George. Fortunately, Jungle was sober. His dad died since I was there last and now he was taking care of his aging mother. Jungle and Crazy didn't know each other from Barstow, but they were kindred spirits. Crazy had heard of Jungle George for years, and he was surprised to find that Jungle was very different from his reputation. Of course, Crazy wouldn't have formed that opinion if he'd experienced Jungle while he was drunk. Not long before we left, we hung around an old house that George was restoring, and in conversation I told Crazy about Jungle getting drunk in New Orleans. Jungle then looked over at me and said, "I didn't know you knew about that."

I said, "Jungle, you trying to hide that is like trying to hide a fire in the dark." Before leaving, Jungle showed us around historic Ft. Scott, including the Civil War era fort where we took pictures of each other in the old jail. I never saw my old friend again. He died in August of 2002 from colon cancer.

After visiting a few more Civil War sites, Crazy ran out of drugs. "Hey Richard, I ain't bull shittin', man, my fucking head really hurts. I'm gonna have to see a doctor."

"Tell the truth, asshole, you wanna get high."

"You can't feel the inside of my fucking head, Richard. I'm the one that feels it, and it fucking hurts, man."

"Well, it's damn funny that you didn't start getting headaches until we made it to Michele's."

"I did. I just didn't say anything."

We found a veteran's hospital, and while we were in the waiting room I said, "You know Crazy, I really don't like spending my vacation hanging around in these fucking waiting rooms so you can get high."

"There you go again."

"Let me put it this way. I don't fucking believe you."

"Well, I can't help that," he said dejectedly. The physician wouldn't prescribe anything good enough to satisfy his craving, so that made him all the more determined.

Between the hospital and my next stop in Tennessee, he did nothing but whine about his headache. I didn't believe him any more than the last doctor did. While listening to him whine, I went looking for Teddy, a retarded childhood playmate whom my grandmother was raising until she died. I found an old man in a barbershop who knew Teddy, He told me that he burned up in a fire some twenty years previous. I then located one of his sisters, and visited with her for awhile before I left.

From there we went to Washington, D.C., and I'm glad that Crazy was able to see the Viet Nam wall. Since he was a vet, he was expecting an overwhelming emotional experience that's so common to vets who visit the wall, but it didn't happen and he couldn't understand why. To this day, I'm convinced that it was because he was too preoccupied with getting something to get high on. Before that, however, when we visited the confederate prison in Andersonville, Georgia, he and I both had somewhat of an emotional experience, which we probably wouldn't have had, if we'd not seen the movie recently. Why at Andersonville and not at the wall? Perhaps he did have a headache in Washington, D.C. Maybe I was wrong about him using feigned headaches in an effort to get drugs, but I don't think so.

In West Virginia Crazy said. "Hey Richard, see that little medical center over there. I have a feeling I can get good treatment over there."

"The only feeling you have a feeling for is drugs. Why can't you admit that?"

"Just go over there, Richard. I don't wanna argue anymore."

That was it, I couldn't take anymore of his arguing and complaining, so I told him that I had no intention of spending the rest of my vacation looking for drugs. I took him to the closest bus station and sent him back to Barstow. I made up my mind that I'd enjoy the rest of my vacation by myself and I did.

In March of 2010 I saw Crazy at an AA meeting. When it was over, we went outside and talked. He needed a place to stay while he was in town so I let him stay at my house. In one of our conversations, he mentioned the headaches he had on our trip and said that he found out what was causing them.

"Richard, it was high blood pressure. I wasn't bullshittin' you."

"Hypertension is the silent killer, Crazy. There are no symptoms."

"Well, that's what the doctor told me."

I left it at that. He was still lying about that headache ten years later.

I sent my granddaughter a post card from all the states. Sometimes I'd drive a hundred miles or so out of the way, just to go over the state lines to get postcards. When the vacation was over, I wanted to say that I'd been in all the states except Hawaii and Alaska. The picture albums I have from my Civil War journeys are awesome. Unfortunately, I don't have anybody who shares my interest in the Civil War anymore.

~

With a masters degree I was qualified to teach in colleges and universities. I applied to Barstow College and was accepted as an adjunct instructor in the psychology department. I also applied to Park University and was approved to teach Introduction to Psychology and Minority Group Relations. Over a period of three years, I taught several courses at both schools.

My AA sponsor, Rich, was working part-time as a counselor at DUI School. With his help and recommendation, I also started working there as a counselor. Each 'client' was required to attend six weeks of educational classes where we covered topics such as the use and effects of alcohol; the nature of alcoholism; the impairment of driving skills; and the consequences of getting a DUI. Clients were also required to attend nine weeks of group therapy where we discussed topics such as the physiological and psychological aspects of alcohol abuse; of positive decision making and goal setting; how to say 'no'; availing of community resources, and 'alcohol and the family'. We also did three individual interviews during the 16-week program in an attempt to determine whether the clients were benefiting from the program. I did this for about 18 months.

After my masters was conferred in 1998, it took about a year and a half before I found another school. One of the schools I researched when I was looking for a masters degree program was Pacifica Graduate Institute. In '96 Pacifica started a new degree program in depth psychology. After reading the flyers coming in the mail about it, I was intrigued, so I went to the campus in Santa Barbara and attended an information meeting where I heard alumni and professors describe the program from each of their perspectives.

Pacifica's 13-acre campus in the Santa Barbara foothills overlooking the Pacific Ocean and the Channel Islands was like walking into fairyland. The campus is small but green with big majestic trees, gardens and orchards. The various gardens and people paths are arranged in such a way as to invite the birds, insects, and animals of the area to make their homes there. I was completely enchanted by the otherworldly atmosphere. Being there was like stepping into a magazine picture. By the time I left the information meeting on campus, I decided that I'd get a Ph.D. there if I had to apply every year for the rest of my life.

One of the requirements in the application process was to submit three letters of recommendation. My sponsor, Rich, wrote one. My friend and former instructor at Barstow College, Dr. Joann Jelly, provided a second one. The third one, however, deserves special attention. He was retired superior court judge LeRoy Simmons.

Judge Simmons was the attorney who defended my uncle Cecil on the armed robbery case. He was also the judge who presided in the Erin Brockovich case. He also portrayed himself in the movie, which was filmed at the courthouse in Barstow. When my daughter and I saw it in the local theater, we were surprised to see the same judge who sent me to prison on the big screen. Judge Simmons wrote the third letter of recommendation.

Five years after my certificate of rehabilitation was granted, in 2001, it was time to use it as an official application to open my case to be considered for a pardon. Again I asked Judge Simmons to write a letter of recommendation. He said that he'd think about it and let me know. A week or so later there was a knock on my door, and when I answered it, there stood the man who sent me to the joint. He said, "John, I'd like to talk to you about the letter you requested."

Once inside I closed the door, looked at him and said, "It's often stated around 12-step meetings that if you really want to know what a person is like, go to their home and see how they live."

"Then you know why I'm really here."

"Well, let me give you the tour. I don't get a chance to show it off very often." I showed him the turn-of-the-century pictures on my wall of my paternal ancestors from Sweden, and then all the pictures of my grandkids. I took him into my study where I have *The Collected Works of Carl Jung* and all of James Hillman's books, plus the rest of my collection of books connected to my education in psychology. In my study, he noticed a picture of me with one of his wife's colleagues at Barstow College. He asked, "Isn't that Dr. Jelly with you in that picture?"

I said, "Yes, and the man between us is the eminent psychologist Dr. Phillip Zimbardo, the man who did the famous prison experiment at Stanford University in 1971." Then I pointed to the picture of me and one of my classmates with Dr. James Hillman, the author of over 30 books, and the originator of archetypal psychology.

From my study, it's a step down into the converted garage that used to be my bedroom when I was a teenager. "And this is my gym," I said. He was impressed. The entire north wall is covered in mirrors, so whenever people step down into the gym area they are confronted with what looks to be a gym twice as big as it actually is.

After I presented the mural on my bedroom wall, I took him into my Civil War library. In there I have a Betsy Ross flag and a confederate flag covering most of the ceiling, and pictures of about 40 Civil War generals on the walls. When we returned to the living room, he handed me the letter and said that he was convinced that I deserved it. Here is the letter he wrote:

November 8, 2001
To: California Board of Prison Terms

As this letterhead indicates, I am a retired judge of the Superior Court of San Bernardino County. I still serve as a judge of the Superior Court in San Bernardino, by assignment of the Chief Justice of the Supreme Court. I served full time in the capacity of a trial judge from January of 1977 until my retirement in June of 1994. My court was located in the city of Barstow, a community in which I have lived since August of 1971.

I first came to know Mr. John E. Smethers in the mid 1970's. I had been appointed to represent Mr. Cecil Reeves on a PC 211 charge [robbery]. John Smethers was Mr. Reeves' nephew. Mr. Smethers was a witness for the prosecution in the trial of that case. I next encountered John Smethers, while I was a sitting judge, when he appeared in my court charged with a drug offense. My recollection is that he was originally granted probation and required to serve 6 months in the county jail as a condition thereof. Subsequently he violated his probation and was given another 6 months by Judge Rufus Yent, also in Barstow. Upon his second probation violation I sentenced him to a term of three (3) years in the state prison system.

I am aware that Mr. Smethers has long since finished all that he was required to do and has now established himself in a more normal lifestyle.

He has pursued education and employment and has adjusted to living in the manner that we hope those who process through the justice system will do. To the extent that probation, incarceration, and parole are intended to provide an offender incentive and opportunity for change of direction in life, the system has worked well in Mr. Smethers' case. I believe that Mr. Smethers has accomplished the objectives we hope those who are subjected to the process will accomplish. He has obtained education and training, outside the penal system, that qualifies him to teach and counsel others. Moreover, he in now doing those very things on a regular basis.

Inasmuch as Mr. Smethers seems to have done all that was expected of him, and more, in terms of rehabilitation, it appears that his application for pardon should receive favorable review. I would happily respond to further inquiry should there be more information that would be helpful to you in reaching a decision regarding his application.

Very truly yours,
L. A. Simmons

My application to Pacifica was accepted and I was granted an interview with Dr. Diane Skafte, the academic vice president. I explained to her after our interview that when universities interview applicants, they usually ask a question similar to this one: "Are there any significant experiences that you've had or accomplishments that you've realized that have helped to define you as a person?" Dr. Skafte didn't ask such a question. Because I was prepared, I asked if I could read to her what I'd written. She said okay, so I read her the following:

I am the quintessence of manhood. Leaping buildings in a single bound and smashing granite to me is mere children's play. I have remodeled university libraries on my lunch breaks, rendering them educationally more efficient. I translate ethnic malapropisms for visiting scholars, I write award-winning screenplays, and I practice time-management to perfection.

I impress women with my sensuous and godlike demeanor. I can pedal bicycles up extreme hills backwards with inexhaustible speed, and I hurl a discuss at distances of five miles with precision accuracy. I am an expert builder, and my sexual prowess is well established with over 5,000 women—having bore children with over half of them. I am also an infamous outlaw in Mexico.

I single-handedly tame biker bars in big cities. I play 15 musical instruments. The Los Angeles Dodgers sought me, and I am the subject of numerous documentaries, which include my expertise on the air velocity of Australian swallows. When I'm bored, I build large underwater tunnels, and I enjoy hang gliding over the Grand Canyon. On Sundays, after studying the complete works of Sigmund Freud and Carl Jung, I fix bicycles for children free of charge.

I have sculpted movie stars and painted beautiful scenery in France. I am a mind reader and an honest bookie and card counter. Professionals the world over drool over my original line of country and western attire. I never perspire, and I hold world championships for arm wrestling and weight lifting. I am not a celebrity, yet I receive 25 pounds of fan mail daily.

Last summer I toured Dixie with a traveling brigade of Civil War re-enactors. I bat 400. My elegant floral arrangements have earned me fame in international botany circles, and children love and trust me unconditionally. I can sling boomerangs at small moving objects with perfect accuracy. I once read The Rise and Fall of the Confederate Government, Moby Dick, and various works of Old English in one day, and still had time to remodel an entire museum in Washington, D.C. that evening. I know the exact location of every food item in all major supermarkets, and I have performed several covert operations for the CIA, FBI and the DEA.

I sleep once a month for ten minutes while driving my car. While on vacation in Iran, I successfully negotiated with a group of terrorists. The laws of physics do not apply to me.

I swam the Atlantic Ocean and didn't get wet. The Rocky Mountains fell on me and I'm not dead yet. I can look up the back end of a cow and determine the price of butter, and occasionally, to let off steam, I participate in the art of Kung Fu. I raise award-winning worms in the Mojave Desert, and I have won bullfights in Tijuana, snow-skiing competitions in the Alps, and I speak ten languages fluently.

I have sung in operas and have played Hamlet on Broadway. I have performed triple bypass surgery, and I have spoken to the elephant. I have six bachelors degrees and four masters degrees, but I have not yet earned a Ph.D. in Depth Psychology from Pacifica Graduate Institute.

To this day, I believe reading that contributed to my acceptance at Pacifica, plus Dr. Skafte sounded impressed with my intentions of someday writing a memoir. It was a five-year program—three years of course work and a two-year clock for writing a dissertation.

Nineteen ninety nine was an important year for me. I started classes in the fall term of 1999, and in August of '99, my daughter gave birth to Jeren, my grandson. She and Kenny now have a boy and a girl and are satisfied with not having any more. I can't think of anything that gives me more joy than my grandkids. I used to feel like throwing up when listening to grandparents carry on about their grandkids. I knew that I'd never carry on like that.

In January of 2000, I was hired at MCLB as a library tech and as an assistant in the Education Services Office. The base library wasn't busy, which turned out to be an advantage for me, because there was time to read the mountain of books assigned by Pacifica's professors every month. Fortunately, the director of Family Services, of which the library was under the supervision, didn't object, as long as I didn't neglect what was expected of me. Rich, my AA sponsor, the librarian, and my supervisor in the education office didn't object either.

I commuted to Santa Barbara and back for my course work at Pacifica. There were three full days of classes a month. Students stayed at a motel in nearby Carpinteria where Pacifica provided accommodations, a few others stayed on campus, and I slept in my camper in the parking lot of the Best Western. We'd shuttle back and forth to the campus in vans because of limited parking space on campus. We ate our meals on campus at a buffet-style dining room.

My first term at Pacifica was as gratifying as my last. I enjoyed every minute of it, including all the reading and writing. At first there were 16 of us who would be going through three years of course work together, but by the second year we were down to eleven. Most tracks had more, usually 25 to 30. We became a close-knit group, relatively free of conflicts and bickering among incompatible personalities. Because of this camaraderie we felt unique.

The in-the-nut-shell definition of depth psychology is the psychology of the unconscious, which is where the *depth* part comes from, as in the depths of the psyche. We studied Jungian and Freudian psychology, with an overall emphasis in Jungian and archetypal psychology. We also studied dreams, cultural issues in depth psychology, ecological and cosmological issues. We took a series of research courses that included our summer fieldwork. We studied literary genres, the depth psychological perspective of the sacred and the imaginal (as opposed to the imaginary). The entire curriculum was tinged with mythology, plus a course in the mystery religions. A course in alchemy as practiced in spiritual and depth psychological traditions triggered an interest in alchemy that I'm still interested in today. In one of the two courses we took in Frontiers of Depth Psychology, three professors offered their perspectives on integrating the spiritual aspects of quantum physics with depth psychology. Especially interesting was how Mike Denney, my dissertation advisor, drew upon his extensive experience as a surgeon to explore the quantum domain of healing.

Fieldwork projects were required during the two summers we were there. After 10 years of attending 12-step meetings, I still didn't understand what members meant when they talked about spiritual experience. To me the phrase was ambiguous because there was no definition. In my first summer's field work, I interviewed AA and NA members who'd undergone self-proclaimed spiritual experiences. The diversity of my interviews was illuminating, and by the time I finished with my research project, my ambivalence was gone, mainly because spiritual experiences are themselves ambiguous. The term can't be defined because of its inherent heterogeneity.

My second summer's fieldwork project was geared toward what I thought at the time would contribute to the research I'd tentatively planned for my dissertation. Because I was investigating the lived experiences of criminalized male drug addicts, I thought I'd be able to use interviews conducted with police, probation, and correctional officers to get their perspectives on this population. When classes resumed the following term, I started putting together a proposal for my dissertation. As it turned out, I didn't use the interview material from the second year's project; however, that project gave me the experience I needed for a pilot piece of research to hone the skills that would help me with my dissertation. To that end I was successful.

The first course in the three-course Dissertation Development sequence in our third year, provided the framework for implementing a research idea and writing the concept paper, which served as the basis for the dissertation proposal. The focus of the first course is working with the candidate's research question, writing an introduction, and outlining a brief review of the literature for the concept paper. We also worked on understanding and mastering the American Psychological Association (APA) publication style.

The second focused on drafting the brief review of the literature, statement of the problem, and method sections of the concept paper. We also learned about strategies and techniques for conducting library research in psychology. At the end of this course, students were expected to have a draft of a complete concept paper.

The third course focused on completing the concept paper and submitting it to members of the research faculty and to the Ph.D. administration for approval. We also discussed the ethical standards for conducting research with human subjects and drafted an application to the ethics committee for approval for the use of human participants. Strategies for publishing a dissertation were also presented. The concept paper was the first big hump, and it isn't uncommon for students to finish their course work at Pacifica before getting their concept paper approved. Because I knew the direction I was going for my dissertation, I was finished with everything on time.

Besides completing the dissertation, we also had to pass a written exam, which I passed on my second try. The exam was considerably more difficult than the one for my master's.

The dissertation committee consisted of three people: a dissertation advisor, a coordinator, and an external reader. Some of us selected an advisor from the faculty while we were still doing course-work. Once the two-year clock for the dissertation started, we officially selected the other members of the committee.

The most important person in the committee is the advisor. Choosing one is like choosing a sponsor in 12-step programs. Compatibility is important, and he or she should be familiar enough with the student's field of interest to guide him or her through the development and completion of the dissertation.

The coordinator oversees the process, coordinates the committee, and ensures adherence to the Depth Psychology program's dissertation guidelines. After the clock has started, the coordinator is available for consultation in setting up the rest of the committee if it hasn't already been done. In my case, the first advisor I selected didn't work out, so the coordinator and the chair of the depth program worked together to find another one. The external reader was selected from outside the faculty at Pacifica. He or she couldn't have taught at the institute, held any administrative or advisory positions there, or been a student there. The reader is supposed to have expertise in our topic of interest and be able to evaluate our work from a scholarly vantagepoint within the discipline.

My advisor, a retired surgeon from the San Francisco area, was also a graduate of Pacifica. I couldn't have found a better one if I'd searched the world over. Though we were worlds apart professionally, we were kindred spirits developmentally. Mike had problems growing up that had paralleled with my life, so he could identify with me in many ways. I finished my dissertation a year after my clock started, even with the delay created by having to change advisors. I managed to finish early because Mike was willing to read, make suggestions, and return my work through email. Usually, doctoral candidates have to send a hard copy of their proposal to their advisor who could take up to six weeks to review and send it back with required and suggested changes. Then it's the same process with every phase until the advisor and the rest of the committee have approved the dissertation. Using that process, completing a Ph.D. program generally takes the full two years. My advisor didn't take six weeks to return my work, he usually returned it to me within a week. I was lucky to get him and be the first person in my class to finish. After all of the committee members approved the dissertation, my next step was the oral defense.

The title of my dissertation is *Scumbag Sewer Rats: Criminalized Male Drug Addicts and the Trickster Archetype.* I wanted to investigate a population of people whom I'd been a part of for over 30 years. From the experience I gained in summer fieldwork projects, I set out to interview people in Barstow, mostly recovering alcoholics and addicts from local 12-step programs. Whereas my focus was on the trickster archetype, I was originally attracted to the *puer aeternus* archetype, so I also included a section on the *puer*. I thoroughly enjoyed the dissertation process, especially exploring the archetypes and how they are personified in criminalized male drug addicts. For me the dissertation was fun. There were still a few hurdles to jump, but after the problems were resolved I ended up with a unique dissertation that I'm proud of.

On 2 February 2004 I gave an oral defense of my dissertation, a tradition and requirement that goes back to when Ph.D. degrees were first instituted. The dissertation committee, the department chair, other members of the faculty and students were in the audience. After I presented my oral defense, the members of my committee asked questions. My external reader wasn't able to attend, but he was allowed to send my coordinator his questions by mail. The only other questions came from one of my classmates and one of my professors. After all of the questions were answered, the committee then retired to an adjoining room. They came back a few minutes later with a bouquet of flowers and a "Congratulations Dr. Smethers."

I have attended the defense of all but one of my classmates. Unfortunately, two of them are A.B.Ds., which stands for *all but dissertation*. For anyone who has languished in that purgatory, those letters might as well stand for 'all but dead.' A.B.D. is the uneasy period between finishing course work and finally being handed a doctoral degree. For many, it looms like an extended judgment day—one that can last for years—before the hoped-for ascension to Ph.D. is earned.

All the education prior to Pacifica was worth the experience of studying there. I loved it. If I had the money, I'd go back for another masters in mythological studies or maybe even another doctorate. I've also enjoyed going back there for seminars and to watch my classmates defend their dissertations. I wanted to convert my dissertation into book form so I hired a consultant to help me through the writing of a book proposal. The consultant served as my proposal advisor like Mike served as my dissertation advisor. My book *Scumbag Sewer Rats: An Archetypal Understanding of Criminalized Drug Addicts* was published in May of 2008.

Although my Ph.D. was conferred on the day I defended my dissertation, the graduation ceremony was held four months later. Only two of my degrees were important enough to me to attend graduation ceremonies: My first one from Barstow College and my last one from Pacifica Graduater Institute.

POLICE RECORD - JOHN SMETHERS

Date	Place	Incident/Offense	Outcome
07-25-60	PD Barstow CA	Broke curfew	Released to parents
08-03-60	PD Barstow CA	Petty theft (Milk)	Released to parents
11-01-60	PD Barstow CA	DUI & broke curfew	1 year juvenile probation
06-15-62	PD Barstow CA	Trespassing	Released to parents
10-19-62	SO San Berdo CA	Petty theft (hub caps)	Released to parents
02-10-63	PD Barstow CA	Open container & possession of alcohol by minor	60 days in jail & 2 yrs formal probation
06-25-63	PD Okla Cty OK	Theft (mayonnaise)	$20.00 fine
07-01-63	PD Toledo OH	Drunk & disorderly	$9.50 fine
10-28-63	PD Barstow CA	Violation of probation	3 days city jail
09-19-64	SO San Berdo CA	Possession of narcotics	120 days county jail & 3 yrs probation
09-09-65	SO San Berdo CA	DUI	Acquitted
11-10-65	SO San Berdo CA	Public intoxication	Released

08-08-67	SO San Berdo CA	Resisting arrest & drunk	60 days county jail
12-04-67	PD San Diego CA	Investigation of burglary	Detention only/not an arrest (3 days)
12-10-67	SO Riverside CA	Pedestrian on freeway & false info to police	$50 fine & 3 yrs informal probation
02-06-68	SO Riverside CA	Contempt of Court	Time served
10-15-68	SO San Berdo CA	Investigation of burglary	Dismissed
01-20-72	SO Las Vegas NV	Possession of marijuana	Dismissed
03-15-72	SO San Berdo CA	Receiving stolen property	No complaint filed
10-23-72	SO San Berdo CA	Petty theft (tequila)	5 days city jail
11-17-72	SO San Berdo CA	Robbery & drunk	Insufficient evidence
12-07-72	SO San Berdo CA	Possession of marijuana & failure to pay fine	Dismissed & fine
12-12-72	SO Los Angel CA	Open container	5 days county jail
12-20-72	SO San Berdo CA	DUI-drugs	2 yrs formal probation

01-06-73	SO San Berdo CA	Public intoxication	Arrested and released
06-15-74	PD N Ls Vegas NV	Public intoxication	Arrested and released
09-29-75	PD Ls Vegas NV	Forged Prescription	2 yrs formal probation
10-18-76	PD N Ls Vegas NV	DUI & Possession of Drugs	$150 fine & DUI school
11-01-78	PD Ls Vegas NV	Forged Prescription	Dismissed
12-02-79	PD Ls Vegas NV	Forged Prescription	$100 Fine
11-10-82	PD Ls Vegas NV	DUI	Fine & community service
08-10-84	SO San Berdo CA	DUI	Sentence concurrent w sales of meth
08-15-84	SO San Berdo CA	Public intoxication	Arrested and released
08-25-84	SO San Berdo CA	DUI	Sentence concurrent w sales of meth
10-26-84	SO San Berdo CA	Possession of narcotics	Dismissed
11-05-85	SO San Berdo CA	Sales of meth	6 months county jail & 5 yrs formal probation
07-14-86	SO San Berdo CA	Violation of probation	6 months county jail
11-04-88	SO San Berdo CA	Under the influence	Dismissed

11-04-88	SO San Berdo CA	Failure to Appear	Dismissed
11-04-88	SO San Berdo CA	Probation Revoked	3 years state prison & parole
04-06-95	So San Berdo CA	Certificate of Rehabilitation	Granted
02-19-10	State of California	Pardon	Denied

www.ingramcontent.com/pod-product-compliance
Lightning Source LLC
Chambersburg PA
CBHW031507270326
41930CB00006B/294
* 9 7 8 1 9 0 6 6 2 8 5 0 5 *